Praise for *Spirit of the Bear Lodge*

Dedicated to Gaydell Collier, a founding member of Bearlodge Writers, *Spirit of the Bear Lodge: A Bearlodge Writers Anthology* is a collaboratively-edited anthology that is both gracefully and thoughtfully organized—filled with carefully selected and well-crafted pieces. In richly detailed imagery and finely wrought language, the works in this anthology reveal a strong connection to questions of place and community. A testament to writing community and writing *in* community, this book brings to beautiful fruition the presence, talent, collaboration, and craft of Bearlodge Writers. This anthology is a celebration of individual voices working cooperatively to further their writerly talents in unison, and it is a powerful and engaging collection.

   —Lee Ann Roripaugh, author of *tsunami vs. the fukushima 50*

Spirit of the Bear Lodge honors the talented writers found in the landscapes of Wyoming and beyond. This collection of fiction, nonfiction, and poetry brings a spotlight to inspiring words. Be stirred by poems, "Given Wings" and "Dream Watch," and get lost in a variety of short stories or essays like "Root Deep." There is an emotion for everyone to capture in this lovingly curated anthology.

   —Jessica Kristie, author & publisher

This unexpectedly touching anthology gave me pause for thought as I read through it. The blend of stories, narrative, and poetry forced me to slow down and examine my perspectives. True artistry of words is contained within this collection.

   —Aaron Linsdau, publisher, Sastrugi Press

Spirit of the Bear Lodge

A Bearlodge Writers Anthology

Gyroscope Press

Gyroscope Press
PO Box 1989
Gillette, WY 82717
gyroscopepress@gmail.com

Spirit of the Bear Lodge copyright © 2023 by Bearlodge Writers
First Edition 2023

Cover painting: Sarah Rogers
Cover design and interior layout: Constance Brewer
© 2023

ISBN: 978-1-7367820-4-0

Published in the United States of America

Spirit of the Bear Lodge
is dedicated to Gaydell Collier

Gaydell Collier was a charter member of Bearlodge Writers and of Wyoming Writers, Inc. She was a sustaining member of Women Writing the West and of Western Writers of America. A woman of great faith, Gaydell was writer, reader, editor, horsewoman, naturalist, librarian, artist, care-giver, cherished friend, and revered mentor to a host of writers.

The important thing is to touch the earth and stand in the wind, to know you are part of a whole – not superimposed like asphalt. On the plains, in the mountains, you learn that you are as important as the beaver, the hawk, the dragonfly – but not more so. You are part of the circle.

Gaydell Collier from *Leaning into the Wind*

Foreword

Good bones. That's what house renovators say old homes need to make them worth saving. This phrase applies to the Bearlodge Writers as well. We still follow the mission and guidelines set forth by our charter members. That framework has formed the basis of a long-lasting organization.

Bearlodge Writers was first envisioned as a place where writers could gather to share, create, and encourage each other. Founding members shaped our "good bones," and though we forge new courses, the echoes of their distant voices stay with us.

The Bearlodge Writers have been meeting bi-monthly in Sundance, Wyoming, since 1979. The Hills have drawn us from different directions. We are ranchers and homemakers, artists and teachers, musicians and business people—but most of all, we are wordsmiths.

We encourage and support one another in our writing endeavors, help each other improve our work, share information, and provide workshops and writing retreats. We produce poetry, essays, novels, short stories, articles, and columns. Our published works ripple outward—regionally, nationally, and internationally.

Our table has changed little in essentials since its founding. We still bring chocolate along with our red pens. We critique gently but honestly. We try to give each other what we need, be it grammar help, publishing tips, or simply non-judgmental ears to listen.

Through writing, in our different ways, we forge new courses. We explore a past that calls to us and query the present for meaning. Sometimes voices answer—be they inspiring, sad, or bittersweet. We seek to pierce the fog, to discover new insights and wisdom through our writing. We strive to relinquish the illusion of control and let words flow, leading us where they will. The pleasure of creating and of sharing our creations generates a thrum of contentment, a safe place where we learn and grow together.

These are times of change. The Bearlodge Writers have changed, too. Our members' homes stretch from Maine to the western shadows of the Bighorns, though our group's heart remains in Sundance, Wyoming. At times, our table has become a virtual one, as we incorporate words like "Zoom" into our vocabulary. In this shifting geography, we aren't always physically "at the table," but our spirits remain there. The essence of who we are endures.

Table of Contents

PART ONE

Forge New Courses

A River's Symphony
by John R. Gutiérrez

The Big Horn River sweeps everything
into its blood-red current.
Flowers and plush green plant life
witness the water's devastation.
Waterfowl float the river.
A sandhill crane stands like a sentinel,
observes the tragedy.
Along the banks,
eggs of sage-hens, chukars, and pheasants
float like small golf balls, spatter yellow
on the bark of the unmovable trees.
Around the bend of the river, both
the cottontail's home and badger's den
are inundated.
A fawn and a spring calf collide;
neither escapes the labyrinth
of dead trees and branches.
Both drift with the current.
Both give in to the killing water.

From the branches of dead cottonwoods,
killdeer and meadowlarks accompany the bass calls
of crows and ravens. Magpies join the chorus
of Mozart's Grand River Symphony.

"War, Peace, and Marriage." *Freedom's Candles: From Tiananmen to Vilnius*
by Jytte Holst Bowers

We were the last children of the Victorian age who curtsied to our parents. We never saw them in their underwear, and we put sugar in the window for the stork so he would bring us a little brother or sister. We were the children of a Second World War, who learned to hate and mistrust before we learned the rules of grammar and the multiplication table.

"When we are free, we will travel. We will cross borders," my grandfather said. "Oh, Little Heart, you shall behold sights you won't believe." My grandfather and I often walked down to the harbor of Copenhagen, and, like the Little Mermaid on her rock, we looked longingly across the water toward the Swedish coast where the lights, so close but forbidden to us, were sparkling. "So much freedom," my grandfather sighed. He dreamed of coffee and butter. I dreamed of chocolate and bananas. In May of 1945, after five years of occupation, we lit candles to celebrate our freedom. They glowed and flickered into the early hours of the lovely spring night, sending the long shadows of war back into the far corners of childhood.

After years of hardship, I wore my first pair of nylons, ate my first grapefruit, and went to my first ball in a dress made out of our kitchen curtains. Most important of all, I took my first trip out of Denmark to Norway, where I marveled over clouds that cast shadows on the mountains. We danced to jazz bands while the bells of freedom still rang in our ears, and lengthened our dresses to fit The New Look; seams which already had been let down several times were camouflaged each time with bright silk ribbons. We chewed gum and collected pictures of Hollywood stars, while we solemnly promised one another that we had seen the last of wars.

***

The words *au pair* had not entered the dictionary when my friends and I went to England to learn the English language. We were simply called *the maids* and learned to scrub floors and pans—although we didn't learn to pronounce the *th* sound. "Oh, oh, there she sinks again; go and rescue her," my employer used to say. "T-H-I-N-K, my dear. *Think*, is that so difficult?" Yes, it is, I thought, as I stood in front of the mirror and tried to put my tongue up in between the gap in my front teeth. After two years abroad I returned to Copenhagen. I stood at the rail of the ship and waved to my waiting family on the pier. I recognized them all. No one recognized me with the thirty pounds I had gained the two years I was abroad. One of the last things taken off the rationing in England was chocolate. I was there when it happened and looked it! The death of King George failed to touch me, but the lifting of the chocolate rationing—*ooh, la la.*

I never did learn the *th* sound. But the years abroad gave me enough confidence to apply for a degree in nursing. "My dear Miss Holst," the matron looked at me over her gold-rimmed glasses, "your record in Physics and Biology leaves a lot to be desired. Hmm, shall we say, quite a lot?" Then she patted my hand. "Your own physics, however, look strong enough."

I sent a grateful thought to Cadbury's and the hundreds of hours I had spent polishing pots and floors. "I will give you a try." With a curt nod she handed me over to the instruction nurse so I could try out a uniform and have a view of my room.

The following six months were a probation period in which our academic work, as well as our performance on the medical floor, was evaluated. I struggled in the classroom, but at the bedside, I was in my element. Eventually, I was able to put the anatomy, biology, and physics together to match the diagnoses, all written in Latin on a small blackboard behind the patients' beds. One morning during the professor's rounds, I touched my head nurse's hand.

"Yulitis?" I whispered and pointed to the word encircled by a small pine branch on the blackboard over a bed where a shriveled-up old man lay with the sheet pulled up to his chin. His eyes anxiously followed the professor, who gave him a reassuring pat on his hand. "Shh, Miss Holst," the head nurse hissed as we passed to the next patient, "I will tell you later."

Later I sat at her desk eager to take notes. "Miss Holst," she said, "you may never interrupt a professor's rounds." I nodded. We had outgrown the curtsying to our parents and our teachers—but to the professors, the democratic ways had yet to break ground. "Now, for *yulitis*, my dear girl; you will not find that word on the test tomorrow. This little old man visited his doctor a few days ago. His cough was minimal, his throat slightly red; but when the doctor found he had no family, no one to give him a Christmas dinner, he admitted him to the hospital. Then, at least, he could get some food and warmth during the season. Ten years ago, while you were still playing hopscotch, all of our beds were filled. All kinds of diagnoses were dreamed up during the night as ambulances darted in and out of Copenhagen picking up the Jews. They occupied the beds until they could be brought down to the fishing boats which took them to Sweden—to safety."

In 1956 I graduated. We were handed our diplomas by professors who thought up words like *yulitis*, professors who thought up diagnoses for hundreds of frightened Jews. We curtsied deeply as we received our diplomas.

***

A World War, peace, and then one more war called the Korean War. As we graduated, a Cold War between superpowers threatening one another with total destruction had left us restless and vulnerable; our idealism had turned to cynicism.

I took a leave of absence from the hospital as I found myself wishing that my makeshift bookshelves warped under the weight of medical books were filled with poetry instead. I traveled to a Folk College far away from the hectic life of Copenhagen to take a three-month course in the liberal arts. I loved every minute—literature in the morning, art in the afternoon. Poetry and painting, music and politics filled the three months of the summer when Denmark is most beautiful. Every afternoon, an hour before dinner, the recent happenings in world politics unfolded up to the very minute. The lecture hall was crammed. One day I found myself sitting beside a student filing his nails. "How rude! Why don't you listen?" I whispered.

"His Mao jacket and Red point of view bore me." He looked at his hands and continued to file.

That evening I was late for dinner. The only place left was beside that rude student.

"You seem quite nice," I heard a girl on the other side of the table say to him, "but I can't understand why you put on such an act when you speak. Do you want to sound different?"

"Maybe it is because I am different," he said and laughed. "Allow me to introduce myself. I am an American. My name is Jim, and I have only spoken Danish for eight months."

The professor continued to wear his Mao jacket. Jim continued to file his nails. His accent became less, our friendship greater, but when the three months were over, we parted. He was going back to his divinity school in America and I to my job at the Children's Psychiatric Ward in Copenhagen.

"I thought you loved him," my friend said and turned to me as we saw him off.

"Could you ever imagine me married to a Congregational minister—smiling and baking cookies in America?" I hissed.

"Don't tell me," I said when I answered my doorbell eight months later and found Jim standing outside. "Let me guess.

Your theology professor bored you, so you sat and filed your nails and they threw you out of Cambridge."

"Cambridge is in England," he laughed, "I was at Yale."

"That's a key, not a school."

"It's a school."

"I wouldn't know that. It's ten thousand miles away, on the other side of somewhere. What brings you here?"

"I changed my course of studies. I decided to study literature instead, and when I left the divinity school, then I had to serve in the army. I'm on leave from Germany."

We spent the day walking up and down the streets of Copenhagen, as easy with one another's thoughts on the cobblestones as we had been last summer on our walks in the forest. Our weekend was followed by letters. In turn, they were followed by a spring wedding in Copenhagen.

Watershed
by John R. Gutiérrez

Mountains sleep, then awaken.
Spring water rushes,
streams join rivers,
dams control flow.

In the flatlands,
floods forge new courses—
no control for the forces,
fierce, fast, and fatal.

Immersion
by Holly Moseley

Incense
  greets the guest immediately,
  invites intimacy,
  expands into eternity.

Breathe
  in…
      out…
  in…
      and out…

Receive
  in lungs, mind, and heart
  the gifts of
  being,
  listening,
  Love.

Root Deep
by Kathy Bjornestad

My love for the forest might have something to do with vacations. When I smell pine trees and the drift of smoke from campfires, I'm immediately transported back to childhood summer trips. I'm riding down a highway stretched out in the back of our old Chevy van, then parked next to a numbered log post near an outhouse and water pump, then tucked within a dusty-smelling tent while rain tap-dances on the patched green canvas. There is a brief and strange camaraderie with other campers, a transitory communion that seems almost magical. Campgrounds are the domain of the rootless, but the trees remind us that some things remain after we go. They will carry on.

I'm a lifelong Tolkien fan, and his Ents speak to what I've always felt about the woods, that they are alive in some semi-conscious way—that lidless eyes watch me pass beneath, and conifers mark time with their rings and wait with endless patience, whispering secrets of the universe to each breath of wind.

Scientifically speaking, trees really do talk, just not with words. They have their own special ways of communication. Beneath Canadian forests, chemical signals scoot along roots, pinging messages back and forth between like and unlike species. I'm hungry! I need more sunlight! Give me water! The hub tree, a gigantic Douglas fir, receives word that its cousin, the leafless birch, requires nutrients. In spring and fall, this tree sends sugar to the birch through symbiotic pathways, and the birch returns the favor in summer. Nitrogen. Potassium. Phosphorus. They thread from tree to tree. Firs cloaked in shade tap into this network to receive missing elements. Those in drought request water, and through this arterial system, mature trees foster seedlings. Stressed trees are succored, and the forest thrives.

Despite drought and bark beetle infestations, despite fire and autumn snows so heavy that branches crack beneath the load, my forest also thrives. In the Black Hills of Wyoming, the ponderosa pines sheath rolling hills in protective shadow. Some places, bare gray branches protrude like finger bones, but mostly, the hills remain an unbroken carpet of dark green that appear black from a distance.

My own roots don't lie at the edge of the Black Hills. I wish they did. I'd like to be as my neighbors, with a many-branched family tree sprung from a single trunk. On some of my neighbors' acreages, family homesteads still stand, half-forgotten in lonely hay fields, stranded a hundred and fifty years in the past. People here speak of deceased great-grandparents with the detailed knowledge of time travelers. They can point out the rose bushes Grandma Betty planted in 1902 or the patch of wild asparagus Great-Great Uncle Russell discovered along the creek bed while panning for gold. In this place, the past walks hand in hand with the present. But it feels like I travel alone, having been transported here from a large city hundreds of miles south.

My forefathers' remains are sprinkled like sawdust across the country. Somewhere in Texas, a small cemetery houses ancestors whose stories are lost to me. On my father's side, cornfields in eastern Nebraska preserve a legacy my great-grandfather created to sustain his descendants. But the farmhouse burned down long ago, and on my own, I'd have trouble locating the 156 acres of rich farmland that remain.

Sometimes I feel rootless. This is not my parents' fault, but the fault of my own lack of attention to the old stories, and to my ancestors' penchant for not staying in one place. I often thought it would be nice to boast of having extended family where I live. Envy tugs at me when my students' grandparents show up at spring concerts and basketball games. When my cousin decided to move to northeastern Wyoming with her girls—*Finally,* I thought! *I will create my own legacy to pass on to the next generation. I will spread my own roots.*

Maybe that's another reason I've always felt so drawn to the forest—imagine the scope of a family spread over an entire landscape. When a tree falls in the woods, it often comes to rest in the loving arms of its kin. Those trunks that do manage to touch earth provide entire habitats for beetles and digger wasps and grubs before finally decomposing enough to nourish the soil. I find reassurance in the knowledge that, each spring, mother pines produce cones, which drop in August or September. While squirrels and birds confiscate many seeds, enough survive to start a whole new generation of seedlings. Next to my house, limestone mining took out many ponderosa pines. Mining companies must reclaim the land, but that doesn't include replanting trees. Nevertheless, what was an empty field when we arrived eighteen years ago is now a nursery of eight-foot-high striplings.

Pine saplings often sprout where the earth has been disturbed, as during road building. Thus, a perfect line of sentinel trees grows along the drive that leads to our workshop. Bordering the road to the house, several more pines stand like guideposts. You'd think we'd planted them with purpose, but our hands took no part in the landscape's re design. In fact, when we tried to transplant a few baby pines on our hillside, they quickly died. Apparently, some things are best left to the trees.

My whole life I've striven to find my way to the forest. Raised on the plains of Wyoming, after college I trudged into the desert to make money, but not really live. After circling the state in dot-to-dot career changes, my husband and I planted our roots in Sundance, Wyoming. My house sits under the benevolent presence of the forest. My apple and crabapple trees bask in the meadow below the house. A lone aspen perches halfway up the opposite hill.

I visited a friend the other day. She pulled back the curtains in her dining room window and invited me to view the flowering apple trees outside. Their white-blossoming branches reached up to greet spring. I envisioned knotty toes curled in black soil as they sunbathed. The old tree couple had weathered life's blizzards and droughts and hailstorms together, silent and stoic. In August, they'd birth bouquets of apples, a single tree's bounty enough to stock a pantry with jars of applesauce—and plenty left over for browsing deer and greedy robins.

Apple trees depend on each other. Propagation requires pairs. A lone tree can't cross-pollinate. Without that second tree and a few busy honeybees—no apples. An apple tree doesn't even need its own specific kindred to create fruit. A flowering crabapple will do. McIntosh, Golden Delicious, Baldwin, Jonagold . . . they are non-prejudicial trees. Their biology knows no racial ties; it only requires water and warmth in equal measure and at the correct times. Oh—and a nudge from the insects. This has been proven by my own single dwarf McIntosh, which in a good year forms fruit thanks to its neighboring, pink-flowered crabapple tree.

Likewise, aspen aren't reclusive, though, on my five acres, only one aspen grows, tucked close against a black oak. Come autumn, its golden leaves shimmer in striking contrast to the oak's burnished orange. What is its story, I wonder, since quaking aspens are supposed to grow in clusters? Did its sisters die? It looks lonely, that aspen, but I need only crest the next hill to discover a coven of blond sisters across the road. Perhaps these cousins know their kin's history, but they aren't talking. Instead, they conspire next to a declivity where water pools after the winter thaw and tiny frogs sing at dawn. Beneath the dirt, I imagine roots coiling outward like electrical wires, twisting in a complex system descended from that first ancient aspen. The oldest known aspen has lived over 80,000 years, always in good company. The aspen's siblings need only copious sunshine and moist soil to rapidly reproduce.

Like my human neighbors, this tree is long-enduring, perhaps because it surrounds itself with family.

Once summer casts her eye across the hillsides, I unearth my hammock and rise to meet the forest. I watch for fallen branches to avoid tripping and keep my mouth closed, since spiders delight in spinning threads between the trunks. Eventually, I discover two trees spaced about ten feet apart and string the hammock. Hugging the trees, I pass ropes from hand to hand and slipknot them tight. The hammock seems too flimsy to support my weight. I straddle it, balance, and sink down. The canvas cradle rocks. Stills.

Needled branches cocoon me in shade. I sway side to side and look up past an opera of color. Sunlight glints through pine needles before clouds shutter the light. I feel the friendship of the forest, the connection of the trees. My roots stretch deep, just like theirs. I, too, was once a sapling. Now, though my children may depart, invisible roots link us together.

Long ago, my husband and I buried our spaniels under two baby pine trees. The older dog, Quincy, died before he could enjoy the five-acre tract of land we'd dreamed of owning during years spent in sagebrush prairie towns. But the second dog, Maggie, loved her walks through dappled paths among the rocky hills above the house, where pinecones crunched beneath my feet and sunshine glinted through dew-wet needles. In the forest, tree trunks stood firm against the press of my palm. I breathed deep the musky, damp earth and was filled with new purpose. I, too, could be strong and green.

Now, looking out my kitchen window, I envision my pets' bones curved into neat piles beneath beds of buffalo grass, their essence seeped into soil where roots feed. Those ponderosa pine gravestone markers where we buried the dogs, once mere seedlings, now tower twenty feet high. Thus, the dead give back to the living.

Humans share over fifty percent of their DNA with trees. We breathe. We reproduce and respire. Consume and excrete. Live and die. When I'm lonely, I remember the promise of the trees. I rise and walk paths the deer have made. Roots twine below me. The sky stretches above, vast and unending. And I balance between.

On warm summer evenings, my husband and I prop lawn chairs next to a fire and bask in the shade by our creek. We dream dreams together beneath the box elders and make plans that may not come true. But that's all right, for our pleasure lies in expectations rather than in results. And when he's gone, I'm still not alone. My current dog—a chocolate Labrador—is always close, lolling in cool grass or sniffing out mice in the woodpile. Families of birds inhabit the boughs above me. Flickers and woodpeckers drum for insects while swallows dive after mosquitos. A squirrel scolds and scampers as he leaps nimbly from branch to branch. Doves coo hauntingly even further aloft, their gentle cries offset by the crows' harsh tones.

When I lived in the city, I was alone. Now, I am a part of a community. The deer, the wild turkeys, the jackrabbit that pauses to eat clover near the house, and me—our lives connect beneath the sloping arms of the trees. Those trees that watch over us. Those trees that provide for us all.

Place-Based Learning
by Holly Moseley

The horizon changes
depending on the light.
Limestone cliffs shine in the sun;
clouds create shadow valleys
or mimic mountains behind the buttes.

I try to learn the lay of the land,
decipher the language of this place,
but it is new every morning,
changes in the afternoon,
shifts again at sunset.

This ancient dirt seems inconstant,
stones sink into earth, then suddenly erupt;
each day, a new geography,
outside my door
and inside me.

Bittersweet
by Patricia Frolander

At dawn she slips through bur oak to the chokecherry bush.
Yesterday's heat dwells in draws, lies in mown hayfields.
From precarious perch, she leans toward the hanging fruit.
Nimble fingers, purpled by juice, strip small berries
into a bucket dangling from her arm.
Bees buzz, sip nectar from late summer flowers.

She casts a glance toward the grassy bottom of the ravine,
remembers a heat-filled day, buckets of berries cast aside,
youth and desire reaping another harvest.

Tears and sweat mingle as she gains the top of the hill,
her gaze rests on the ranch house in the distance.
By now the nurse has cleaned and fed him,
his recognition never comes.

She hopes he's calm today,
wonders if his vacant mind
remembers the taste of chokecherries.

PART TWO

Echoes of Distant Voices

Attic
by Morgan Callan Rogers

I swear I could jump from the top of the attic stairway
down to the hall of the second floor. Thirteen stairs.
"Watch," I begged my sister. She stood at the bottom, "Don't
do it!" But I did it, because I could fly.
I remember it just that way. I truly flew. I did.

We lived in a three-floored house until I was eight.
The attic on the third floor had two finished rooms.
Our scattered toys ruled one room. Maple dressers
and a double bed took up the heart of the other room.
My sister slept beside me. I didn't sleep at all.

I waited to be bombed by B52s from a nearby base.
The show before *Lassie* had me convinced
we were at war. We would be buried in rubble.
I roused my sleeping mother, who told me,
"Go upstairs and go to sleep, for pete's sake."

One night I sleep-walked and woke up in the toy room,
next to a large, walking doll with one arm. I stared at
her fixed eyes, petrified. When the cold in the floor
seeped into my back, I scurried back to my sister,
who slept through my night terrors and wanderings.

During the daytime, my sister and I walked through a passageway connecting the two rooms. We scaled
a half wall in the middle—dropped down into eaves,
where we jumped up, and scared each other. *Boo!*
You didn't scare me. Yes, I did. You did not. I did!

First grade now. Playing with girl classmates in the
toy room. Girls formed a circle around one and moved
in a rosy, shouting, "Poor! Dirty!" The girl in the circle
cupped hands over eyes, weeping. Outside the circle, I
shouted, "Stop!" I swear I did. I did. I remember that.

We moved when I was eight years old. I tucked
a small toy into the darkest corner of the eaves; a yellow
plastic giraffe I named Vanilla. I hope a sweet, terror-free
child clutched that giraffe in her small, feisty fist,
heedless of loud, growling planes cruising overhead.

Home Alone
by Jytte Holst Bowers

When we went into the third year of war, the word *babysitter* had yet to find its place in the Danish dictionary. There wasn't much money for entertainment, anyway, so parents stayed home with their children. The German occupation forces declared a curfew on Danish citizens. People had to be back in their homes by eight in the evening, if not earlier.

So when Aunt Sophie's invitation to her nephews and nieces arrived to attend an all-night party to avoid the curfew, there was a lot of excitement. Aunt Sophie adored the younger branch of the family. She was a generous birthday and Christmas giver. And they adored her. Why not? Especially when you could hardly get anything in the stores—and even so, everything was on coupons. Aunt Sophie owned a small wine and tobacco store in one of the small streets close to the center of Copenhagen. She was the only member of the family who could let the wine flow and the cigarettes burn as if there was no tomorrow. Her invitation certainly could chase the ghosts of war away for one night.

"Of course, you should go," said Cousin Lilly to my Uncle Niels and Aunt Gertrud. "Jytte and Nora can stay with us. We are far from Copenhagen. Nothing ever happens out here. Inger and I can take care of Nora, and Jytte can help us." Lilly, at sixteen, was certainly responsible enough, and her sister Inger, fourteen, had just been confirmed. I was eleven and considered our youngest cousin, Nora, at six, a mere baby.

We felt very grown up as we waved goodbye to our parents. They promised to return on the first train from Copenhagen the following morning. We settled down with *pandekager*, a thin blini rolled around ice-cream and strawberry jam, before we started to play a game of Parcheesi. Nora had just learned the rules, so we didn't laugh when we sent her men back to home base.

"What are they doing up there?" Lilly jumped up from her chair.

"Who, Lilly?"

"The German soldiers. We never have soldiers out here; they are too busy in Copenhagen."

We looked out the window and saw four of them marching back and forth across the viaduct. Bayonets were slung across their shoulders.

"They are looking for something," I ventured.

"Well, what do we care? Your turn to throw the dice, Nora."

"Turn off the light, Inger," Lilly whispered when we heard a knock on the front door. "It might be the soldiers. Shh, be quiet; we are definitely not opening the door to any Germans."

The rapping on the door became louder. Now, it sounded as if they were kicking with their boots. Finally, it became quiet. Lilly put a comforting arm around Nora. "Don't cry, sweetheart; they have gone, but we had better not turn the light on." We crawled over to the window. In the twilight, we could just make out the two soldiers returning to their post.

"Let us pray." Lilly was leading us in the prayer we all knew from heart, but for Nora. That night she learned it. "Let us say it once more." Lilly was very authoritative. We all held hands.

"Will they come and get us?" Nora sobbed.

"Of course not." But Lilly's voice sounded a little shaky. "Let us pray once more."

I had never prayed so much in my life, but the German soldiers were still marching. By now it was almost dark. It was difficult to see them.

"Ca . . . ca . . . can't we turn on the light?" Nora stammered.

"No, no. We turned it off when they came to the door. They know we are here."

"I have an idea." After a while, Lilly had broken the quietness. "We can go down to Bette. We can crawl along the path. The trees will keep the soldiers from seeing us."

Bette was the wife of Lilly's and Inger's grandfather. He had divorced their grandmother years ago in order to marry Bette, causing bitter strife in the family. After their grandfather's death, it had softened a little, but she was still not welcome. The family gathered around their real grandmother, a little withered woman who after her divorce always wore black. She was considered the head of the family.

The grandfather and Bette had both been well-known artists. Their small cottage was filled with easels and unfinished works, for Bette lost her spirit after her husband died. She didn't lose her house, however. Lilly and Inger were allowed to visit her. She never crossed the threshold of their home.

Nora had begun to cry again, and Lilly was determined we all would be better off if we were with Bette. So we crept down the front steps onto the narrow path down to her home.

"Wh . . . what in the world made you come here?" Bette's voice was high-pitched and shaky. "If the soldiers had seen you, God only knows what they would have done. Of course, you can stay. It will have to be on the floor." Nora's smile returned; Lilly was convinced we had done the right thing.

"I heard earlier," Bette continued, "that the Germans are expecting a train with weapons heading up to Norway through Sweden, and of course, they are expecting sabotage. They will probably stay on the railroad bank until tomorrow. Well, let me get you settled for the night. For sure your parents will get it from me when they come home in the morning."

I thought I heard a little tone of triumph in her voice.

Encompassing Noise
by Constance Brewer

Wind through the pines. Ringing in my ears.
Both persistent. I came to the mountain to think
about who matters but all I hear are tones
in my head—subtle whir of a fan, slosh of waves,
call of one distant bird whose cries never cease.

Voices outside my head can't compete.

The sound of my parents arguing is the steady
rise and fall of word swallows headed to the barn.
He had expectations, my father, that my mother
would care for him in his old age, his Parkinson's.

My mother's bee of resentment buzzed
in the background, until one day, silence.
The making of honey fell to my brother,
the one who stayed.

I am like her in all ways that matter save one.
Left with an insistent low drone loop in my head,
it drowns incomplete thoughts at birth,
expectations tiny bee corpses at my feet.

Semper Fi
by Jean Helmer

When our daughter and her husband relocated to serve a church in Arizona, we began making regular treks to Phoenix. Our first Sunday there, we were welcomed to church by Dick Taubert, a 90-plus-year-old parishioner who sat in a rear pew watching for newcomers. As was his custom, Dick introduced himself and invited us to sit with him. By our second visit, we joked about being a "pew family," and our daughter invited him to join us for a family dinner. On the Sunday of our third season of snowbirding, Dick invited me for coffee with the Friday morning group of lively people in their eighties and nineties.

On the appointed day, I arrived at the parking lot just as Dick was removing his walker from his SUV.

"Good morning," I called to this tall, upright man.

"It's a beautiful day, isn't it?" Dick replied.

He easily kept pace with me as we approached the church door. His speed was remarkable considering his ninety years and the stroke he'd suffered. I stepped ahead to open the door for him. His chin jerked upward. Reaching over my head, he grasped the door.

"Ladies first," he said, nodding to indicate that I should precede him into the building.

"Thank you, sir." I smiled at the formalities honed into him during an earlier era.

There were eight at coffee this morning. Conversation waxed and waned, and gradually turned to downsizing and the difficulties of deciding what to keep and what to toss. Everyone had a story. At last, Dick spoke.

"I have a small chest that I kept," Dick said. "It's traveled the world with me. Got it when I was 17 and joined the Marines. Had it with me overseas during the war, back in 1944."

At the mention of war, the conversation turned to children and grandchildren currently deployed. Silence descended, cocooning each of us in our own thoughts, then resumed as we shared cake and a second cup of coffee. As the gathering ended, I volunteered to do the clean-up. Soon, only Dick and I were left in the room.

Dick's mood had been subdued since he had mentioned his chest. As the others left, he had stayed in place, seemingly waiting for something. His walker sat behind him, against the wall. Finally, he rose, pushed in his chair, and stood gripping the chair back. His head drooped, and then he raised it slowly and made eye contact with me.

"I opened that chest." He paused. His shoulders sagged. His head hung low. After a moment, he raised his head and stiffened his jaw. "You see, there is a journal in there." His eyes locked onto mine. "I hadn't forgotten about it. I knew exactly what it was and where it was. And I knew what was in it. A man doesn't forget a thing like that."

Dick sagged into silence and bowed his head. His age-gnarled fingers kneaded the chair back. I waited in silence until he straightened and spoke.

"That book has a roster of my men from the war. I was a sergeant and was responsible for fourteen men. While I had my house, I had a flag that I flew each day. And I had a little ritual that I did every day. In the morning, I would raise the flag and then greet each of those men who served with me by name. Now that I'm in an apartment, I don't have a flag outside. I have had to change things, but I still do my ceremony. It is my way of honoring them. It's harder now, though."

His voice trailed off. He again bowed his head. I waited as the silence grew. At last, Dick straightened his shoulders; his posture became military stiff.

"That book has a cord that holds it shut. I opened it, and I wish to heaven that I had not. You see," he fixed me with a stern gaze, "I had remembered all those names. I know them as well as I know my own. But before," his voice faltered. "Before. After," his voice became ragged. "Since I opened that journal and saw those names," his voice trailed off. He inhaled, firmed his jaw, and continued. "Now I see their faces. I hear their voices. I wish to heaven that I would not have opened the journal."

In the ensuing quiet, his pain was palpable. I could think of no words that might afford him comfort. I waited, remained in silence with him. At last he began anew, his voice at once intense and soft.

"I was in the Japanese theater during World War Two. We were in Palau, offshore of a small island, Peleliu. That was something, trying to get on shore. You see, the Japanese had planted railroad ties into the seabed during low tide. Then they strung barbed wire around them. Couldn't see them at high tide. When we were going in, the soldiers had to crawl over the wire to gain access to the beach. The Japanese were entrenched with machine gun nests. The men climbing over the wires were easy targets."

Dick's head sagged. His fingers tightened on the chair back until his knuckles turned white. After a moment, he continued. As he spoke the memory into the air, he was no longer addressing me.

"Once we got across those wires, we ran into a sea wall. They had stacked coconut logs four to five feet high just beyond the tide line. Again, we became easy targets. Anyone going over the wall was silhouetted against the horizon. That was all it

43

took. They just picked us off. After a while, we came up with a plan. We waited until between 2 and 3 a.m. We all lined up and went over in a single wave. You see," Dick's jaw grew rigid. His eyes pierced mine. "It was the best chance we had … the only chance we had. They couldn't shoot us all."

I nodded slowly at the inevitable wisdom of the tactic.

"We lost more than half in that landing." These words, forced out, carried a sorrow that had not diminished with the years.

This time I could only shake my head as what he said registered. This time, it was my head that sagged. Just as I thought he was through speaking, Dick resumed.

"We had been taught some Japanese. Well, really only a phrase. It was something that meant 'surrender,' but they didn't teach us anything else about the language. We had managed to work our way pretty deep into this small island. There was a machine gun nest up ahead. We crawled through the bushes. The shooting was coming from a cave. I crawled to the mouth of the cave and yelled the phrase. There was more shooting. I yelled again. More shooting. And again, with the same result. Suddenly I realized that someone was crawling up beside me. One of my men was tugging on my foot. I glanced away from the cave's mouth to see what the soldier wanted.

"Say it soft. Say. It. Soft," the man told me.

"Soft?" I asked him.

"Say it in a soft voice," the man repeated.

"You see, this fella knew a little bit about the Japanese language and how it worked. So, I did what he said. I said the phrase again. Before, I had been shouting it at the cave. This time I said it soft. This time there was no shooting. I repeated the phrase again in a soft voice and waited. The shooting

44

ended. After a while, the Japanese surrendered. The soldier explained to me that when the phrase was said loudly, it meant something like 'Come out so we can blow your heads off.' But, when it was said in a soft tone of voice, it meant 'please come out so the shooting will stop'." He paused, eyes focused far away. "They should have told us that."

Dick straightened, turned, and pulled his walker into position.

"It would have been a good thing to know earlier," I offered quietly, then stood to walk with him as he returned to his vehicle.

Dick took a couple of steps and then swung his walker back to where we had been sitting. "A few days after we took that island, MacArthur got there. I never did like that man. Had no respect for him. He came up to us and told us that taking that island had been unnecessary. That small island was not important to the cause. We lost 5000 men in taking that island, and MacArthur said it was 'unimportant'."

I could not hold back the gasp that flew from my mouth.

Dick nodded slowly. "Unnecessary. Unimportant to the cause," he repeated and swayed slightly with the weight of the memory.

I stepped forward and hugged him. For the briefest of moments, he let himself sag into my embrace, then straightened. He gave a nod, grasped his walker, and moved forward.

An honor guard of one, I accompanied Sergeant Taubert, waited as he stowed his walker and took his place behind the wheel, stood at attention as he circled through the parking lot. He headed west, toward the retirement center, returning to his quarters, returning to his trunk, returning to his journal with its roster of voices and faces.

I remained frozen in silent tribute.

Semper Fi.

***

Footnote from history: I offer this in memory of Sergeant Richard (Dick) F. Taubert and the men whose names he recited daily. The necessity of this World War II battle for control of the Island of Peleliu, also known as "Operation Stalemate II," continues to be argued in military science classes. Admiral Nimitz, Commander in Chief of the United States Navy, believed that control of Peleliu, a tiny island in a chain of islands located in the sea lane off the coast of Taiwan, was essential. The island contained an airstrip and an estimated 500 caves where Japanese troops were entrenched, outnumbering the American troops three-to-one. General Douglas MacArthur, commander of the United States Army and rival of Nimitz, disagreed. The Battles of Peleliu and of Iwo Jima were the two bloodiest battles of the Second World War.

After his death, I learned that Sergeant Taubert was the son of WWI Marine hero Albert Taubert, recipient of awards for heroism in France and Haiti. Albert's second Navy Cross credited him with the attack that resulted in the death of Benoît Batraville and "the practical suppression of banditry throughout the Mirebalais District [in Haiti]." The feat had been internationally heralded.

When World War II began, Albert demanded that son Dick, then a junior in high school, quit school and join the Marines. And, at seventeen, Dick did.

Dream Watch
by Patricia Frolander

I softly call your name as I slip into the stand of wheat,
fifty-five acres of gold.
Careful not to shell the seed, my aged hands
push ripened stems aside.

You must be here, for you love the fullness of a crop.
Yards further, I call again.
The hawk above must wonder
at the trails through the field.

Did you leave with the winnowing scythe,
the burning heat of August?
For some good reason, I cannot find you here,
amid the nightly dreams and tear-damp pillow.

You Are Born into Someone Else's Story
by Bruce Roseland

My father worked himself into an early grave
worrying about things that never happened.
The word "dread" was his constant saying.
He dreaded this, dreaded that,
always hearing ice cracking before the crack,
always anticipating iron to break
but couldn't get himself to weld the fissures
before the snap.
Frozen into the in-between of fleeing or fright,
never enjoying every day blue sky.
If you were a neighbor or casual friend
you could walk away
from someone who's got problems.
No need to be around
a stick in the mud, a doom and gloomer.
Kinfolks would be gingerly, keeping their distance.
But when you're under the same roof,
there's no getting away
from the background noise
of never finding answers to problems,
just the ever on and on drone
of the same old, around & around of what to do,
not much different than dogs
chasing their own tails.
Every so often, like a clay pot
dropped from any kind of height,
things break.
Exhaustion sets in, nerves fray.
My father would just sit in a chair,
worn down to a shell of himself
from not eating, not sleeping,
unable to walk out the door
to do work he knew to do,
totally unsure of himself.
This became time to cart him off

to the nearest psychiatric ward,
in days when they plugged you in
with a wooden dowel between your teeth
and let electricity flow between pads
clamped to sides of your head,
and when you wake up, you've forgotten
your name, forgotten whatever
bothered you before.
My father would be out of his rut,
into a new space.
After a week or two, he was sent home
with pills that put a glaze to his eyes.
But oh, he was driven to get back to work,
twelve hours a day and never a word said
about why he'd left.
Until the unwinding began again,
same old dogs chasing same old tails,
same ragged edge of unresolved fear
digging its ruts deeper, until he would be
sitting in the same kitchen chair, fists clenched,
eyes confused, hunched forward.

When I became of age to drive,
I would be the one, at least once a year,
to take him to the hospital,
then a week or two later, pick him up.
Over time the pills changed,
but the outcome did not.
The hardest thing in life is dealing with
what cannot be changed.
Either you stay or you go.
I stayed.
All things end someday, at the grave,
tidied up with an epitaph,
date of birth, date of death.
The rest of us go on,
picking up a piece here,

picking up a piece there.
I wish I could say
there is a way back, but there isn't.
What is past is past.
I had to turn the page
beyond what could have been,
learn to love the ones I'm with,
live my own story.

Ukraine by the River (a translation)
by Viktoriia Peterson

I walk along the river.
Through the melted snow,
childhood memories emerge.

A wide river
with steep banks.
You could walk for hundreds of miles
and never see its end.
I used to go fishing here with my father.
I remember everything as if it were yesterday.

Now, my father is no longer in this world.
His memory floats like clouds.

In Ukraine,
on the Northern Donets River,
we used to wait for the spring pike together.

Many years have passed.
Fatigue is slowly disappearing.
I will follow the path that remains
as if I were continuing a conversation with my father.

El Dia de los Muertos
by Maria Lisa Eastman

On All Souls Day
we pause, turn,
look out to the hills.

We slow our quick steps
to tenderly open the gate
so *los antiguos,* the old ones,
they can ride in
to bring back our stories.

August hinges moan their rusted song
of almost-forgot swing,
corral rails rest waiting,
pole upon pole shaped strong
hace one-hundred years since.

We are ready.
Esperamos, we wait,
with the sun hot on our backs.

At last a long breath of wind exhales
una brisa, a breeze, from afar.
It carries all the familiar songs,
fading in and out
like the old, the loved.

Ghost horses rise up sudden,
a tight bunch busting
over the long hill.

They gallop,
bringing *los muertos,* the dead,
who ride like smoke,
like dust, like sky
they sweep into the corral.

Outside we lean looking,
our eyes sparkle as
time-carved *calaveras,* skeletons,
slip trembling to the ground.
They greet us, smiling.

Long tails flow,
ancient clothing flutters,
the warm wind frees
tissue thin threads, all
tiny pieces of our history
float near us
like *mariposas,*
butterflies—
we remember the colors,
we remember the fables,
we catch them from the air
and say them out loud.
Our words give them flesh
so that they will land,
so that they will rest,
briefly
aquí, here,
among us.

Piper Dream
by Patricia Frolander

The runway is gone, overgrown with grass and weeds.
Robert's hangar was the first to fall—
tin roof collapsing into the void
followed by each metal side spilling into the open front
where he once taxied his life savings.

The others fell the same—folding in upon themselves.
Now the hoe, plow, and truck have done their duty,
no trace of yesterdays. His Piper, the neighbor's Cessna,
the Beechcraft long-ago sold, the men forgotten.

Echoes of *Clear*! The thrust of engines as they caught,
the deafening roar, wind purged from propellers—
only a light breeze tips the grass,
the silence more deafening
than thunder when planes lifted into the blue.

La Guitarra
by John R. Gutiérrez

The day she was introduced, I fell in love.

I learned to play her over Dad's shoulders,
reaching over, playing rhythm
while Dad played lead.

We laughed and cried with such joy.
I learned her tone, her key and notes,
played her and listened to her songs,
her mesmerizing voice hypnotizing me.
Dad's success was on the fine strings,
Mine, on strings whose voices were thick.
When a song was mastered by us both,
the next time we reversed, so I could boast.

We knew the day would come when we would part.
In my arms, the Silverton, black and white, laid,
Dad kept the Harmony for himself his very first,
Later on, we parted ways Dad and I.

I still recall the day when together we played,
until our fingertips ached.
It hurts my heart that now we don't
for his guitar was long ago lost.

Still, I see that Harmony, Dad's and my first love,
and wish for those days,
to play over Dad's shoulders,
he, the lead; and me, the rhythm on that guitar.

PART THREE

Bittersweet

Scars
by A.M. Hummel

Storm clouds roil over the little cemetery as I watch, just inside the edge of the trees, unseen, and away from the crowd. Could be somebody'll catch it farther on, but this storm will hit here too, in Wyoming's Black Hills, though there's already been troubles enough.

Whole town's come, or what's left of 'em. They've just buried the Sorenson twins, not yet two and dead from the pox. They'll be the last taken. Everybody else is on the mend. There's one more funeral service scheduled, when this one's over and done and those two tiny, scarred bodies are in the ground. It's another twin died.

Mary Sorenson walks alone down the muddy path back to the Light of Life Church. Her Ed's been gone a month, too many others with him. But Mary's got another child, back to the house, still needs attention. Funny how the pox takes some, leaves others of the same blood untouched. Mary moves like a woman suffering hell's torments. I know the feeling. Buried both my own a month or so back. Leaves you numb.

I've helped where I could, whether the fever struck the little ones or their folks. Don't matter much to me. Whenever old Doc Clark come to my place and asked, "Marlee Wallach, suppose you could lend a hand?" I put aside what I was doing, grabbed up my doctorin' bag, and followed along. My kids, Jake and Sue Ann, was half grown and could be trusted to care for themselves, and certain other things that needed caring for, at the time. At least, I thought it so.

I ain't no nurse, understand, but I got a way with healing. Learned it, and more, from Granny. She tended me—me and Momma that is—when we was sick with the pox back in those red clay hills of Georgia. She's the one spooned sassafras tea and aconite into us; wet us down with a liniment she fixed up from sulfuric ether, aqua ammonia, and muriate of ammonia. She knowed to rub our chests with Croton Oil and Tartar emetic ointment, drawing the terrible scarring pustules away from our faces, to our chests. Worked pretty well on me . . . not so well on Momma.

Granny was there, again, after Momma died. She and Poppa clashed regular, sometimes about his "Anderson bullheadedness" being cause enough for Momma to take her own life; sometimes for the things she was learning me. Katherine didn't take to Granny's teachings, but for me they've been real handy. 'specially when something like this pox comes along. Works opposite, too. People forget the good I've done them. They look at me funny; I can almost hear what they're thinking. They stop their discussions over coffee and homemade pie at Barnhart's Café when I walk by, look knowingly at each other, and do this thing with their eyebrows that pretty much gives their thoughts away. Some even do it at church services.

Didn't cause me particular bother until my kids come home from school upset because the others was teasing 'em. That happened after I took in a couple of boarders. Had to make ends meet, but sure set tongues to wagging. Bad enough to be thought of as a witch-woman, worse yet their whispering of low morals . . . or none. Well, what the townsfolk don't know won't hurt them anymore. Or me.

Weren't long after the gossip started that the schoolmarm paid me her visit. Wanted me to keep my two to home, said they was a "disruptive influence." My Jake and Sue Ann, and them the best-behaved in her classroom! She brung some books by, told me to keep 'em studying for as long as they had the interest. Said they could go far . . . that's what she said. Sue Ann was heartbroke, had been real close to Miss Eliza and wanted to be a teacher when she growed up. Jake? His dream was the U. S. Navy. Where he got that, who knows. I'd considered Eliza my friend, too. Maybe 'cause we had common roots in that red Georgia clay? Maybe 'cause she said she thought I coulda done better.

Granted, there had been plenty hanky-panky going on at our place just outside of town, but it wasn't of my doing. Josef sought us out on the occasion, always looking for a steak and a good meal. When he was here just last fall, Charlotte Greenfield, a flashy one if I do say so myself, come home from that high-falutin' school her pa, camp superintendent at Nahant, sent her to back East. Didn't take her long to catch Josef's attention, and vice versa.

Not that similar hadn't happened before, but I'm far past complaining. The first time Josef strayed, just after Jake and Sue Ann was born—they was twins, too, like the little ones they're planting out there now—was with my own sister, Katherine. So much for Poppa's planning. He shoulda married "perfect" Katherine off to Josef Wallach. They was better suited. Guess he figured he'd save the best for last, catch a rich one for the beautiful daughter and increase his holdings. But he jumped on the first offer that come for me, the "imperfect" one, the one who bore the scars from the pox.

Anyway, Josef came home one evening, been drinking heavy, and crawled into bed beside me. Got real tearful and said he'd never do "it" again; said he didn't mind the scars, that he knew I was a better woman than Katherine was. Didn't say much else before he collapsed, more on my side of the old bed than on his own, and commenced to snoring. Left me wondering, but pretty much knowing, just what "it" was he'd never do again. Come morning, he was all lovey-dovey when he ventured out to the kitchen for breakfast.

Next payday? Same thing happened. By then, word was getting around in Kansas City that Marlee Wallach was out kicking up her heels with handsome Josef. Some said it was good, that it was time I loosened up and learned to laugh the way my beautiful twin Katherine often did. Those who cared said it was strange two girls could look so much alike and be so different. Smiled and shook their heads, they did, wondering aloud just how anyone could tell us apart, 'cept by the hair and the paint. Katherine was always real good at doing herself up to be fetching, 'specially if there was a good-looking man around.

They didn't wonder long, though, 'cause soon after the talk started, Josef just picked up and left. No one knew for sure where he went, but there was whispers he'd been seen off in the Black Hills, prospecting his own gold since it looked like he'd be a while in collecting on Old Man Anderson's stash.

Then, it was Katherine left. She made a big deal out of packing her trunks and boarding a Pullman—with its own toilet, would you believe?—drawn by a smoke-belching Union Pacific engine heading out of Kansas City and routed toward "Chicago and points East." Kissed Poppa and told him to hold on to her half of the inheritance, his "perfect" daughter would be home soon, at least for a visit. I got word from a friend of mine, a month or so later, she'd seen Katherine in Gayville, South Dakota. Wondered what she was doing in such a God-forsaken place as that.

I did okay, raising the kids alone for a couple of years, then moved back in with Poppa. Kept house for him for the roof over my head and the place he offered my kids at his table. Katherine came dragging in, once in a while, usually worse for the wear and not saying much about where she'd been. Always playing Poppa's little girl. Always sucking more money outta him. Spending her half of the inheritance, she'd say, laughing, as she packed her bags and boarded that outbound train again.

Josef stayed away. Poppa vowed, unsuspecting as ever, he'd change his will and leave it all to dear Katherine, then that bastard who wouldn't come home and take care of his little family wouldn't get a cent. I didn't much care, one way or the other. I didn't miss Josef anymore, and the kids and I stayed clear of my sister when she did come around. Poppa doted on her; he tolerated me. I was the "imperfect one," the one who reminded him of how he'd lost Momma. And why. Always beating up on himself for letting the scars matter.

When Jake and Sue Ann was about ten, Poppa died. Most figured the drink had finally got to him. I let it sit at that. But before Poppa took that last phlegmy, coughing breath he called his lawyer in and they made out that new will. Copy for the lawyer. Copy for the bank. Copy for Katherine. I was s'posed to get her papers to her. For that, Jake and Sue Ann would get "a little something."

Never rains but it pours, some say. Josef decided about then it was time he got hisself home to us. I didn't tell Josef that Poppa had changed his will, that Katherine and the kids would get the Anderson holdings, so he assumed half was still rightfully mine . . . that making it his, of course. Things went okay for a while, but he got restless and maybe a little more greedy, and decided he'd move "the little family" up to the northern Hills to be with him while he dug around looking for that gold he was always sure he'd find. It wondered me, but fool that I was, I figured he was just ready to settle down. Turns out he'd gotten word Katherine was tending bar in Hill City.

I found them together, my sister and Josef, one night. In what you might call a "compromising situation." Packed myself and the kids off to this logging camp at Nahant, figuring I could do some cooking and washing for the men working the sawmill, if naught else. There were no ifs, no ands, no buts about my leaving, still Josef came all the way out here to Wyoming after a few months, making his usual promises. Was then he took up with the superintendent's daughter, running off in the night when it looked like there was a hanging party being planned in his honor.

That's my story, 'cept Katherine wandered in several weeks ago in the dark of night, already burning with fever. I didn't know then she was bringing smallpox with her, but those first pustules told the story right soon. She said, when she wasn't out of her head, she knew I could tend her because I'd made it through the pox that had all but killed Momma. Asked me not to let her be scarred up the way I was, though.

Things don't always turn out the way a person asks.

Jake and Sue Ann went down real quick. I worked harder on doctorin' them, granted, but the fever burned them bad and they was gone within hours of each other. Katherine lingered for a month and more, finally looked like she might make it through. Had even begun to eat a little of my cornbread, soaked in milk to make it go down easy. She died, coughing up that bloody phlegm, in the back room of my little place, just the night before last.

Josef rode in yesterday on a fancy black horse with a silver-studded saddle. Two ornate saddlebags, hanging heavy with his findings, were draped over the horse's rump. Josef was looking for Katherine, and sotted drunk. He did a lot of ranting about how he wanted Katherine Anderson and how the others had meant nothing to him, not even Marlee. Especially not Marlee. Said, too, that he wanted that damned Anderson money, every bit of it, 'cause he'd put up with enough hell from Old Man Anderson and his woe-begotten twins that he deserved it all.

I didn't say much at first, just let him get the yelling outta his system. He never asked about the kids, or me, but I saw him smile when he sneaked a look at the body I was preparing for the funeral. He stumbled to the door, said he was going out for a few minutes to take the saddle off his horse and to give the animal a drink. Was him wanting the drink.

Josef come in all lovey-dovey, commented that I was looking sorta pale, but he guessed I'd had my hands full through this pox outbreak and didn't have much time for making myself beautiful. Said he was hungry, though, real hungry, and asked if I could maybe heat him some water for a bath and fix him up a mess of greens and fatback—and maybe some of that good cornbread poor Marlee used to make—while he got cleaned up a bit.

I had to smile when he kissed me on the back of my neck and whispered things to me he figured Katherine would expect to hear. I slipped away to the back room, tucked up my hair in a kinda fancy do and smeared a little of her paint on my face.

Then, while he was scrubbing up, I pulled some fresh greens from the garden and throwed 'em into the pot with a big hunk of fatback. Made the cornbread just the way he liked it, too … but with a couple of ingredients Granny used when the occasion was right.

Now, Josef's waiting there, at the next grave site, and he'll play the sorrowing husband. He'll toss that first fistful of dirt on Marlee Wallach's wooden casket after it's lowered into that fresh-dug hole. Those who've come for these funerals will pat his shoulder and offer condolences and say what a good woman Marlee Wallach was. Then, I expect, Josef will mount that flashy black horse and come back to my little shack looking for Katherine Anderson, and her inheritance, and those bulging saddlebags he left under my bed. But they'll all be missing; I'll be gone.

And, Josef is already coughing blood.

Given Wings
by Constance Brewer

We count backward
on both hands the number of people
who touched us in the past.

The grasp on an arm, pinching slightly
in the guise of friendliness,
wanting to add import to the words,

squeezing hard to make their point.
Behind us hands rest on
shuddering shoulders. We long to shrug

out like a horse from beneath a rider.
Index finger a harsh jab,
demanding we get our act together,

sometimes in our face, shaken
with rage to admonish a transgression
we weren't even aware we'd made.

The middle finger response to honest
words spilling before thought.
Ring finger with diamond slid on

then taken off in record time.
Pinky swears.
A thumbs-up of silent approval.

Clapping for others in hopes someone
will clap for us.
Cupping a lost bird in both palms,

feeling the feathered heart flutter,
feet scrabbling at takeoff,
a cipher flying into the world.

Hazelnut Macchiato
by A. M. Hummel

I don't care much for being a woman alone.

My mother-in-law embraces widowhood
and the infirmities of age
with grace and power.

My mother battles the inevitable
with a "no way in hell" vengeance,
declares war,
pouts and spouts and sputters obscenities
to make us laugh.

They're both afraid.

When do I
gather memories,
move to an apartment
where I'll be closer to shopping and people,
hospitals and family?

Life is bittersweet …
tastes like a husband too much loved,
tastes like hazelnut macchiato.

Playing With a Princess
by Jytte Holst Bowers

My mother must have been driven out of her mind that summer when I was in my tenth year. Normally I spent the six weeks of vacation on a farm in Jutland, that part of the mainland jutting north from Germany, the rest of Denmark being a series of islands not yet connected by bridges. During the German occupation, we children were sent out into the countryside for our own protection. But the German military who were occupying our country had put mines in the seas surrounding the Danish isles; so here I was, homebound for the summer.

My parents worked it out so I could take swimming lessons with my cousin in a lake ten miles from home. One day I started out on my bicycle in the early morning hours. As I was passing a cozy old thatch-roofed inn, one of the landmarks of our town, I got off to walk up the hill and was stopped by a young lady in a blue dress covered by a white apron. She had a white, starched cap on the top of her black hair.

"Could you do me a favor? To teeter-totter with Princess Elisabeth," she said. "I am too heavy to do it myself."

"P..p..princess?" I stammered and followed her into the garden.

Right enough, there sat a girl a little younger than I with the blond, curly hair I so often had seen in pictures of her. She was sweet, just like the princesses in my fairy tales, and her face lit up as I stammered my "Hello."

Yes, I was light enough that she could bump me. I in turn bumped her and wondered if her blue blood would show up on her fanny.

I was ten minutes late to my swimming lesson and was scolded by my teacher; there was a sour look on my cousin's face.

"I teeter-tottered with Princess Elisabeth," I whispered to my cousin.

"Oh, what a tall tale that is!" she snorted.

"No, it's true."

My parents believed me. As a young boy my father had been given an apple by the Crown Prince, who was the same age as my father. My grandmother had put it on a shelf where it lay until it rotted.

We were a small country besotted by our royal family, even more so in the middle of a World War. The following morning, I made sure I passed the old inn just at the same time. My weight might be needed for another bumpy ride. On the third day I passed the castle to see if I could get a glimpse of my new playmate. Elisabeth was nowhere to be seen, but her father, Prince Knud, was walking his terrier.

"Can Elisabeth come out to play?" I shouted.

"What is your name?" he replied. I told him.

His next question was the one usually expected in the Denmark of those days. "Where does your father work?"

"He works in the china factory here in town."

So ended my short friendship with royalty, and I didn't even have an apple to show for it.

Truth Will Rise
by Kathy Bjornestad

"I'm telling you, *nene*, you got to see this. It's a real, live tree. *Un arbol* like in the old vids!" Jandra's voice crackled in Raf's ear. She beckoned.

"Liar," said Raf through his com. He swam beneath a fishing net with a flick of his fins. He wore an ORB helmet that supplied him with oxygen. So did his sister. The ORBs looked like beach balls resting on their thin shoulders.

Jandra drifted ten feet below in the warm ocean water. Behind her, their family's seafloor pods squatted amidst a garden of sea cucumbers, anemones, and kelp that swayed in the current. A light shone in the kitchen window.

She flicked off her Bluetooth. "Take that, then," she hissed, her voice reverberating inside her own ORB helmet.

He nudged her on the shoulder and signed. *Sorry.*

She made him wait a few seconds before tapping the Bluetooth back on. Raf was her twin, but her opposite, too—a boy, and therefore inferior. She glared at him, fruitlessly, since he couldn't see her expression through the shaded screen. "Come on, thcn, I'll show you."

Jandra swam away from home, above oyster and clam cages, around the scallop nursery, and under lines of pale green kelp that stroked her back with soft tendrils. Ahead, the water turned from navy blue to bright turquoise. Sea turtles grazed in sandy pastures below them. The sand bumped up against a sunken wall: Havana's Malecón. Past it, fish wove in and out of salt-whitened old buildings in the drowned city.

Raf's voice spoke in her ear. "We shouldn't be this close. If Mama finds out, she'll put us on larvae duty for a month."

"Who will tell her? You?" Jandra shot back. She rounded a pocked dome which must have been some important place once and kicked to the surface. A gentle current rolled past on its way to a gray shore littered with blocky, green-slimed ruins. The sun's brown eye peered down at them, filtered by a hazy sky.

Raf popped up next to her. "Well, *chacha*, where is this tree, then? Or are you luring me into trouble?"

Jandra stroked toward the buildings until her foot brushed against the monument of General Antonio Maceo. The underwater warrior sat atop his rearing horse. She pulled herself up onto the steed's marble neck. "There."

Raf bumped against her. He started to speak, then fell silent.

A short way off, mud swelled above the ebbing tide. Stuck into it upside down was a plastic palm tree bleached almost white. Broken glass lights outlined fake fronds. Perhaps it had once decorated some tourist attraction with a fanciful name like *La Bella Fontina*. At least, Jandra liked to imagine so. The rest of the skyline was as dead and ugly as a giant's gawping, broken-toothed grin.

"Come on, let's go home, liar." Raf fell back into the water.

But Jandra stayed behind. Instead of the satisfaction of a trick well-played, sadness rose in her. It came from some deep, mysterious place only her heart remembered. It would return there. It always did. Until then, she'd stay above, where the ocean had a voice, and once, maybe, real palm trees had waved in the wind like flags of hope.

Coyote Plays Ball
by Morgan Callan Rogers

Friday night traffic halts at red lights. Out of the glare,
Coyote trots fast from one side of the street to the other.
Draws a straight line down a dim cement sidewalk.
Leaves black scat in a crooked crack. Been here, it says.
Saunters past fenced backyards that will not pen him.
Dogs growl and bark; cats hiss and crouch in the grass.
Coyote ignores the mutts and bypasses the pussies.
Follows his own quirky compass down a muddy path.
Lightfoots it through a dark baseball field. Deposits scat
between second and third bases, sashays along left field.
Slips through a small gap in an old chain-link fence.
Dark brush wraps around him and he squats for the night.

Morning baseball game. Umpire, first to arrive, spots scat.
Cleans it up with a used tissue. "*Sumbitch*," he mutters.
Curses as he thinks about his five lost lambs. Adds umph
to his 'YER OUT!' when a bad batter whiffs three balls.
Foul or fair doesn't mean nothing to Coyote. Life is not
a series of innings to him. His world neither wins or loses.
Eat or be killed, nothing in between. Does what he does
without remorse. Catch or be caught. Grand slams only.
When the last lights go out and beings have left earth for
their paradise or somewhere else, Coyote will send out
last pitches to an empty planet; a world series of yowls
to ricochet off the universe and come back to him, empty.

Good Intentions
by James Bowers

Zhou Shaio Peng had hoped to become a student at Beijing University at the beginning of the Cultural Revolution (1966-76), but the universities were closed, and he was instead exiled into the countryside to learn from the peasants what life was really like. Fortunately, he was able to leave rural China in 1980 to pursue his studies in the U.S.

We were graduate students together at Columbia University and became close friends. Joe, as I called him (although in fact Zhou was his last name), lived off campus in a single room shared by eight other Chinese students. His thick, black hair crowned the smooth face of a baby, but he was no child. The intense brown eyes radiated intelligence, determination. His well-worn clothes covered a thin, skeletal frame nourished by rice and little else. He dreamed of a great future for his beloved homeland, and I began to share that dream.

Soon after graduation, I was elated when the opportunity opened up for me, personally, to become part of the realization of that dream. I was hired by the United Nations Development Programme to explore the possibility of making microloans to peasants in Sichuan Province in China. It was amazing to see how much peasant women could accomplish by establishing their own businesses in their local communities with as little as $50 or $75, how they could rise above the daily grind of ceaseless labor just to find enough food to keep their children alive.

Upon my return to the states, the first thing I did was to see Joe. I had failed miserably and had to talk to someone who could help me understand. I was living with my mother in Branford, Connecticut, and invited him to come up for the weekend.

Behind her house was a small, wooded area whose trees had not yet been felled to make room for new houses and condominiums near the seashore. We sauntered along a pathway often used in my childhood where the azaleas were just exploding into bloom, their red petals outlined against green, leathery leaves. The moist, rotting oak leaves exhaled a pungent scent, the promise of new life forming underneath, shaded from the sun's insistent heat.

There was no expression on Joe's face when he sat down on a fallen log to listen to my story.

"When the cadre in Shanghai met me at the airport in their blue Mao jackets and sharply creased pants, I was really impressed by how smartly dressed they were. It was the coolies in the streets on the way to the hotel who were wearing Western-style suits with broad lapels made of cheap polyester."

"If they were dressed in Mao jackets, they were probably members of the Communist Party," said Joe.

"Although there on behalf of the United Nations, I was treated as an academic and taken to the faculty club of a university, which also served as a hotel for visiting dignitaries as well as members of the Communist party. My room reminded me of one I had stayed in in a cheap motel in Minnesota: two single beds with straw mattresses on squeaky springs, a desk and straight chair, not even a shower in the bathroom."

Joe smiled. "But you have no idea what elegance that was for your hosts," he said. "At home they probably slept on straw mats on the floor of a two-room apartment, grey concrete floors, walls and ceilings, no heat, a public latrine down around the corner for their use."

"No kidding? Well, they certainly served up enough food at the banquet that evening. All kinds of special dishes placed on a lazy Susan in the center of the table. Had no idea what it was we were eating, but everything was really delicious. There's one thing that surprised me—no rice. Of course, at the end of the meal, they did offer to serve me some. I was so full that I really couldn't eat another bite, but I accepted it anyway. Strange, though, I was the only one who ate any."

"Well," said Joe, "that wasn't the wisest thing to do. At such a banquet eating rice is to show disrespect toward your hosts. It means you have not had enough good food to eat. Incidentally, that meal was paid for by the state. An ordinary meal for a student is a tin bowl of rice with a ladle full of vegetables, perhaps a piece or two of meat, on the top."

"Wouldn't you know. What a fool I was. Only trying to be polite. Well, in any case, it was on the boat on the way up the Yangtze River that I first became aware of class distinctions. As a foreigner, I was assigned a first-class cabin on the deck with two single beds. A gate of iron bars halfway down the deck protected me from the ordinary riff-raff, but not from the stench that emanated from the communal latrines. As far as I could see, the second-class rooms were filled with bunk beds."

"As a matter of fact," Joe interrupted, "those who were in second-class took turns sleeping in the beds, probably three using the same bed."

"I'd hate to think of what the conditions were for those traveling below deck then. In the dining room, I was surprised to find myself eating alone behind a discreet screen, as if a foreigner were a plague whose Western ways could not be allowed to spread among the general population."

"But you had no idea of the possible consequences for any Chinese citizen to be seen conversing alone with a foreigner. During the Cultural Revolution . . ."

Joe rose, and we began to walk again, slowly, heads bowed. There was a long silence before he began to speak again.

"Many of the students had become Red Guards dedicated to following the wishes of Mao Tse-tung. My father had been a high official in the local government, but he was out of favor with the Party during that time, so he was seldom at home. Some of the Red Guards searched our home, looking for him."

He paused and looked straight ahead, eyes filled with sadness and fear, as if he were seeing some ghost from the past. Several minutes passed before he was able to continue. "Then one day when I was wandering the streets I saw a procession of flag-bearing Guards followed by several trucks filled with 'bourgeois enemies of the state.'

"In one of them was my father, hands tied behind his back and lifted up so that he was forced to bow his head in embarrassed submission. A school chum was next to me. 'Wasn't that your father?' he asked. 'No!' I shouted and hit him in the face. My father was being taken to a concentration camp, better known as a school for reeducation through labor." By now Joe had regained control of himself.

We sat down again. I tried to change the subject since it was obviously so painful for him.

"Look at those stunning azaleas. I don't recall seeing any in China. Do you have them there?" But Joe was not to be dissuaded.

"Sometime later I was able to arrange to meet him at a crossroads outside of town. I saw two men coming toward me behind wheelbarrows filled with heavy rocks. It was not until one of them came up to me and kissed me on the forehead that I realized he was my father."

"My God, how awful! What happened to him?"

"After the Cultural Revolution he returned to his old job to work alongside those who had sent him to the camp. There was no such thing as private ownership of housing, of course, so he was responsible for doling out the limited supply of apartments to a long list of supplicants who had applied for them. He was constantly at odds with his co-workers, insisting that housing be apportioned only to those on the top of the list. They wanted the apartments to be given to their relatives and personal friends."

Joe's lips became taunt, grim. "He was sent to a Party conference as a representative of our city. On his return, he discovered that all the apartments had been assigned to his colleagues' relatives. He became so agitated that he had a stroke and died on the spot."

I didn't know what to say. His face was an inscrutable mask. To put my arm around him would probably have offended him. I started to stand up again, but Joe appeared lost in a world of unutterable misery. In the end, all I could think of doing was simply to continue my story.

"Well, hmm, at the quay in Chong Quing the Mao jackets were again there to welcome me and to take me to another educational institution, this time one connected with the shipbuilding industry, which I thought a bit odd. Why would they be teaching how to build ocean-going ships in a city hundreds of miles up the river from the coast?"

"That's because during the Korean War Mao expected the American army to invade China," Joe explained. "Many essential resources, including important academic institutions, were moved away from vulnerable cities along the coast. His plan was to allow the Americans to invade the coastal area, then drop atomic bombs on them."

"I can't believe that!"

"Well, that was the rumor going around at the time."

"In any case, I had scarcely settled in when a delegation of provincial officials appeared. Through an interpreter, I explained the concept of micro loans to peasants and presented statistics to prove how successful the program had been in other countries. The delegation listened in silence. I thought I had made a pretty good case for the project, although I realized we would have to start out on a small scale.

"On my journey up the river, I had seen thousands of rice paddies being plowed by teams of oxen and each plant placed in the soil by hand in the centuries-old tradition. Surely officials wanted to raise the standard of living for a least some of these wretched peasants. But there were no questions asked, and another banquet was held in my honor that evening."

By this time, I was filled with despair. "I thought we really could begin to realize your dream of a new China."

Joe picked a sprig of azalea from a nearby plant and coddled it carefully in the palm of his hand. It was the same vibrant red as the flag of his beloved China.

"Several days later I was informed that the local police would not let me travel into the rural areas, for security reasons. I was allowed to visit various parts of the city, accompanied by my interpreter to make my stay more pleasant."

"And to keep an eye on you, of course," said Joe.

"At last a seat was found for me on a flight back to Shanghai, and I was escorted with great courtesy to the airport. Joe, what did I do wrong?"

"Nothing. You simply didn't realize that the peasants are under the absolute control of corrupt local Party officials. To give money directly to the peasants would undermine their power. The officials you met never had any intention of allowing

Westerners to interfere, despite the interest in microloans some members of the central government had shown."

"I guess I will never understand the Chinese."

Joe gently took my hand, turned it over, and placed the azalea in my palm. "No, you never will."

Ode to a Miller Moth
by Maria Lisa Eastman

My favorite shirt is sky-blue plaid
with long cuffs, pearl snaps.
A tiny silver thread runs through the cotton
like the quick glimmer of trout in a high mountain stream.

This morning, I picked up my shirt,
out fell a miller moth, and he was a fat one.
Brown and black, he lay quiet on the floor.
Perhaps he thought he was still hiding.

I scooped him up, tossed him out under the trees.
Millers are tough, not like butterflies, whose wings
you must not touch, lest you brush off
their magic dust, crippling them forever.

Yes, it's true, millers can take some handling.
This gives them a chance, however slight,
to survive the grip of a grizzly bear,
who makes meals of them—tens of thousands.

Hatching in farm fields each spring,
millers grow strong, darken the sky,
in a fluttering eclipse, they travel to high mountains,
alighting at last above tree line, across talus slopes.

Once arrived, millers do not like
the fiery sun, crackling dry air,
they creep down to the cool, dark rock-belly,
where all grizzlies know they may be found.

I've seen those bears at their unlikely feast—
they move haltingly, flip refrigerator-size rocks
with one paw, and keep the other free to scoop
great clumps of astonished moths into their mouths.

One or two millers may drop free,
stutter off on startled wings,
but most return down into their unlucky asylum.
Perhaps they know it's their fate to nourish, not to escape.

Still, in late summer I see a lucky few back home,
peering through window screens,
crawling under a silver-threaded shirt,
to be discovered by me once again and

tossed out under the trees—
out, out, out into the air.

A Return to the Weeping Willow
by Jytte Holst Bowers

"What did you expect to see—a group of Holsteins grazing by a creek?" Lilly was obviously annoyed. She had a right to be. I had insisted on using my last day in Denmark to go to my aunt and uncle's farm.

"It's not a farm any longer. It has changed hands about three times since you were here last. I know that you will be disappointed, but if you insist, we'll go."

I did, and we drove bumper to bumper for almost two hours on a three-lane highway, the same road we used to travel by bike from Copenhagen in less time, with fewer obstacles.

"Where is the small forest we used to ride through? The one with all the anemones?"

"Goodness, did you say you came from America? One would think you came from Russia. Aren't things in constant turmoil over in God's own country? It's fifteen years since your last visit. We've joined the European Market, the Global Market—small farms are out, and big businesses are in."

"Oh, I'm happy that Hamlet's Castle is still there. What if we couldn't say that 'something is rotten in the state of Denmark' any longer?" I forced a small laugh as we came to a halt in front of the farm. It was no longer a farm, but a restaurant with a big sign advertising platters of cheese, red wines, coffee, and desserts.

"Yes," Lilly looked at me, "What did you expect? Holsteins drinking out of the creek that carried our small peapod canoes into a future our wildest fantasies couldn't even predict? Let's order a cheese platter and a glass of wine so we can toast to a tomorrow of wealth, stress, and dissatisfaction."

A cowbell, the last memory of the Holsteins, clanged lively as we opened the door. A young girl, blond and very Danish, took our order.

"Would you like to sit inside or out?"

"Out, by all means, by the willow tree at the end of the garden."

"Goodness, we cut that down years ago; how could people find us if we had left it standing? Tell you what, the stump is still there with a tabletop. I'll bring your order down there. How did you know about that tree anyway?"

"When we were small girls in the middle of a war, our arms used to encircle it." Oh, what was the use of telling a young university student what had been: about a forest of anemones replaced by high-rise apartments, an old farmhouse demolished to become a profitable restaurant, a willow tree turned into a table and a group of Holsteins who had left only one bell behind.

I lifted my glass to Lilly. "What a wonderful vacation you have given me. I think that I am ready to go back home tomorrow."

Oh, I reflected, this was the first time I had called America home. It was where all those I loved now lived.

I took Lilly's hands. It had been fifty years, and then some, since all our secrets were hidden behind the willow leaves.

"Let us see if we can encircle the plastic top," I laughed, "but first tell me, where will the children hide when all the big trees have fallen?"

PART FOUR

Pierce the Fog

Baptism
by Patricia Frolander

She stands by the open Kansas grave,
baby sister held in her twelve-year-old arms.
No tears yet for her mother lost,
or stepmother in the crude pine box below—
no time for sorrow.

Milk four cows, skim the cream,
churn butter, feed the baby, the chickens,
clean the soddy,
launder by washboard, haul wood.
Dad gone for weeks looking for work.
Neighbors haul cream and eggs to town,
ask her how she and Daddy are doing.
She says, "We're fine,"
although she's terrified of every night alone.

Her salvation's the Bible,
not because she believes in God anymore,
but the stories carry her each day.
She's Daniel in the den fighting
the rooster with spurs as wide as her hand.
She's Noah when the rain falls for four days—
the prairie sea grass floats until the sun devours
the moisture and then she's Jesus in the wilderness
but she doesn't call upon God to save her.

Her grandmother does—
takes her home
gives her and sister a bed with a mattress,
food, warmth, sanctuary.
A brief hug and pinafore on Christmas
release tears held too long.

In winter firelight Grandmother reads
about salvation.

November, The Pirate
by Morgan Callan Rogers

November, the pirate, taking no prisoners, all swords and
swagger, kicking through the October's trick-or-treat debris
and seizing a bounty of silver and gold.

November, leaving last summer's spotless fawns standing
naked within the twisted bones of a tangled thicket,
and about to learn life's lessons with a bang.

November, the heartless hussy who steals a boyfriend because she can, only to throw him out by the side
of the road begging forgiveness, and cold.

November, the distant, private aunt no one really knows,
pushing a clothing tag down the neck of a garment
to save an unaware wearer's dignity.

November, the roommate who rises early and brews fresh
coffee before she clears up last night's raucousness, eager
to celebrate the clean slate of a new day.

November, revealing an old dog moving in her autumn gait
around a bend towards a gray-haired woman admiring
the elegance in the stalks of bleached wheat.

November, flicking a golden-edged leaf from a cottonwood
down into the thinning strands of the woman's silver hair,
making her cry out as it pierces her heart.

November, guiding the dying through hospice and into the
arms of another season, where unearthly light shines, and
cold silence reigns over resurrection.

Prom Night, 1964
by Jean Helmer

The night of my junior prom, I went only to the banquet. I joined friends at linen-covered tables in the armory-gymnasium that had been transformed into an undersea world. Twisted crepe paper streamers in three shades of aqua dropped from wires stretched between basketball hoops to the floor where they were taped securely to the court's boundary lines. In strategic locations, stage walls from the drama department formed two sea caves. One served as a backdrop for photos and the other backed the temporary bandstand. In a corner formed by the arched bridge entryway, a blue whale spouted a live stream of water. I had been on that committee. We were proud of our chicken-wire and papier-mâché sculpture. It took hours to get it to look like a whale. That challenge paled during the trial run of the recirculating pump. We discovered that adding water to tempera painted papier-mâché reduced our efforts to a soggy mass of newspaper strips drooped across chicken wire. We started over. Our second whale was more cartoonish. He was heavily enameled and shellacked. Seeing our masterpiece now actually performing as imagined was the highlight of my evening.

I found the name card designating my seat at a table with other dateless teens. After a welcome and a grace had been delivered from the head table, sophomore servers began delivering our meals. The menu centered on chicken cordon bleu. We approached the dish with trepidation. Cautiously we cut into the rolled chicken breast. Exchanging glances, we looked carefully to determine what ingredients were hidden inside. This was foreign fare compared to that served at Watt's Finer Food Café or at the A&W. We tasted tentatively. Not bad!

The emcee announced the conclusion of the banquet. A teen tidal wave swept out the doors leaving to change into tulle, taffeta, and ties. They would return in about an hour for pictures and for the pageantry of the Grand March. Then they would two-step and jitterbug until the 2 a.m. breakfast, prepared by parents and served at the local Vet's Club.

I joined the tidal wave flowing out of the gymnasium, hopped into my parents' Rambler, and headed west. Twelve miles later, I parked in the garage and walked to the house. While my classmates changed into flowing formals, I changed into my work clothes and barn jacket, and grabbed the big flashlight. While boys escorted girls across the arched bridge into the undersea world of the gym, Herman, our collie-setter mix, escorted me across the frost-firmed mud path worn between the house and barns.

Twelve miles east, a crowd of parents watched from the shadows. The juniors and seniors and their dates stepped into a circle of spotlight where, in a rite of passage, they were formally introduced to the beckoning world of adulthood. I stepped into the corral. A crowd of heifers watched me from the shadows beyond the yellow pool of light coming from above the barn door. I shined my flashlight beam across each heifer, spotlighting them, looking for signs of impending birth. A couple of heifers had withdrawn from the others. I walked around each of them in a circle. Hooves, transparent through protruding water bags, announced birthing times were approaching. The heifers would need to be checked in two-hour increments throughout the night. We could not afford to lose another calf.

While my classmates turned into the arms of their dates and began gliding to the music, I reached down, patted Herman's head. He leaned against my legs. Together we listened to plaintive coyote songs coming from the hills in the back pasture. Together, we returned to the house. Once there, I shed jacket and shoes. I poked my head into my parents' bedroom. The room was dim, lit only by light from a living room lamp, light which spilled across Dad. His cancer was taking its toll on all of us. Mom sat on a dining room chair she had placed next to Dad's bedside, listened for each labored breath. She dozed while she waited to see if I would need help with the livestock. I tapped her shoulder, roused her from her semi-sleeping vigil.

"Everything under control?" she asked.

"Got feet showing on two," I said. Mom looked exhausted and haggard. "You better lay down before you fall down, Mom."

"Guess so. If you'll check them at midnight and two, I'll check at four. That'll give us both a little sleep."

I grabbed a book and settled into Dad's chair near the lamp in the living room. At the midnight check, I looked for the two heifers. One had given birth. Her still wobbly calf was sucking, his tail happily wagging.

At 2 a.m., while my classmates were entering the Vet's Club, I was re-entering the corral. My flashlight quickly found the second heifer that I'd identified on my first trip. She was lying in a corner away from the others. I flipped the beam of my flashlight on her, watched as contractions rippled through her body. The calf was well on his way to being delivered. After a few more contractions, there was a quiet whoosh. The heifer stood, turned, and began licking amniotic materials from her calf's nose. I waited until the calf found his feet, then headed to the house and bed. And thus, the heifers, their newborn calves, my classmates, and I made our way through one more rite of passage, moved one step closer to the thing called adulthood.

Eulogy for a Plain Black Cow
by Maria Lisa Eastman

In the dusk of a long day
we walk tired horses in
one last check of the herd.
But something is wrong.

Out in the grass we can just see
a motionless mother cow,
legs akimbo, belly risen lifeless
in the day's deepening light.

We ride out to look
and slowly turn away.
Full-on dark now—
tomorrow we'll settle with her,
find her calf, hoping that another,
heavy in milk, will claim him.

That night, I dreamed swirling water
wrapped cool arms around her,
carried her soundlessly to the sea.
But in the new day, she remained.
The tides of my sleep
hadn't shifted her body,
hadn't swept her away in timeless surf.

We approach to bear her
soft as we can out
to the sagebrush hill, to rest.
Her family, friends, all stand,
shoulders touching, liquid eyes
absorbing our solemn task.

With bellow and boom,
a requiem rings, heads swing,
their warm mass opens,

revealing a perfect bare-earth
circle around her great form.

Breathless, our dismay
thins with wonder—
even we can recognize
the split-toe signature of grief,
their eulogy sung in muddy plainsong
through the night.

Gulf Shrimp
by A.M. Hummel

I should have packed
      before Wyoming's blizzard warnings posted,
      before temperatures bottomed out,
      before the last rain measured froze
      and broke the rain gauge.

My sun is warm.
Salt permeates my memory.

Waves crash,
      gulls skree,
      a foghorn sounds and a trawler,
      box-full and homebound,
      breaches the front, cuts wake
      in blue-green water.
      Gulf shrimp are fresh,
      not frozen.

This woman,
      whose mama tried raising "belle"
      and got "cracker,"
      tires of ice
      and of age,
questions bravery,
challenges reasons not to compare such
with stupidity.

I am too many years away.

On Our 50th Anniversary — 16th May 2009
by James Bowers

You and I are dead, reborn as We,
To pierce the fog of all hypocrisies,
To see with eyes unblinking, face to face
The sorrows and the joy our hearts must face.

For they are both the same and beat as one,
The ecstasy of love, the birth of son
Who humbles us with joy and pride again
While straining to transcend his ravaged brain.

My academic mind, your heart made pure
By doing what we must, though not so sure
That others understand our true intent,
Not to be false, say only what we meant.

These bodies must soon fade to dust, unseen
That we be One, as we have always been.

Diving into Grief
by Jean Helmer

My left brain
reels at the suggestion
of diving back into
the dark memories of January.

                              My right brain insists
                    knows that I cannot go forward until I have
                              entered Grendel's cave of grief
                                    faced the monster
                                    of death by suicide.

                    For six months, I have
                 refused to acknowledge the reality,
                       refused to think or to feel.
                            I steel myself
                 to drop backwards into memory's abyss
                 to sink through the darkness of sorrow.
                 I know it will take me to the cemetery
              to January's mud, quick-frozen with questions,
           to the man double-tapping a one-knuckle farewell
                 onto the gray coffin holding his brother.

My left brain staggers
unwilling to delve into the brackish waters
unwilling to stir the sludge of memories
unwilling to let me write, think, or feel.

                              My right brain instructs:
                       "Take a long, deep breath. Hold it.
                    Tumble backwards into the dark waters.
                    Yield to the blackness. Sink to the bottom.
                    Land feet first to escape disorientation."

        I sink through the funeral to the visits from his classmates
              bringing questions to their old English teacher.

They ask:
"He was more than a student wasn't he?"
"He talked to you a lot, didn't he?"
"It was kind of like he was your kid, wasn't it?"

I analyze
I could have returned his calls from the bar
I should have recognized the difference
between drunk and depressed
If I would have … just one time

Only when I confront reality will I begin to heal
I take a long, deep breath, hold it, and tumble backwards
into sorrow's sea.

Feathers
by Holly Moseley

Emily once said, Hope is a thing with feathers
but I find it more like sunshine.
Some days are full of warmth and light.
Other days, when the sun is dimly hidden
behind clouds and circumstances
and despair creeps in like fog,
hope feels cold and gray as the day.
Harder still are harsh days:
heat beats down, energy drains away.
When hope demands my all
I must learn to carry it lightly,
like a feather.

Seventy Sparrows
by John R. Gutiérrez

> *"In war, memories are made. Some we forget.*
> *Some we cannot."* —Eleanor Rice

I met Eleanor, a lady of eighty years of age, in the summer of 2009. She and her husband were annual camp hosts in the Big Horn National Forest of Wyoming for most of the summer. A friendship was established, and early in the relationship we were able to easily share information concerning mutual values, morals and our faith. Trust and confidence sprouted and grew between us. This helped nurture an environment in which the sharing of intimate conversations about our lives more confidently and safely occurred.

The strongest thread that kept us tied to each other in this woven net of ours was that both of us enjoyed fishing. We took pleasure in fishing together and competed with each other as to who would catch the first fish, the biggest fish, and the most fish. We often joked about who was a better fisherman. Eleanor most often out-fished me and won in all of these mentioned categories. My being a good sportsman and a not-so-bad fisherman allowed me to continue fishing with her even though I didn't triumph much of the time.

In several of our conversations, Eleanor recounted her experiences when she was but a young girl. One of the most enjoyable conversations to listen to was a series of experiences that took place upon her immigrating to the United States when she was twenty years old. She arrived in New York City where she quickly adapted to a new homeland and started her journey toward becoming an American. After achieving the goal of graduating from college, she quickly found a job as a chemistry teacher instructing non-traditional students at night. Her second job was working in a factory where many of these students worked alongside her during the day. A few years later, she met the love of her life; they married, moved to New Orleans, and raised two children, a son and daughter.

I got to know this amazing woman quite well. On one occasion, she told me about an event I'll never forget. As she recounted this incident, she cried. Her tears touched my heart, and I cried. This is Eleanor's story.

I was barely ten years old but remember well when the Germans invaded Poland. Back then, my father was a farmer, and his land provided a good living with little or no difficulties for our entire family. My mother stayed at home and did small jobs to make a little more money for our essential needs. Being the youngest of seven children, three brothers and three other sisters, made for a tightly knitted family. My oldest brother John was married and worked as an accountant in the city of Warsaw. He and his wife had three children, and after a few years in his new profession, he bought a small house outside the city. My brother James lived in the outskirts of Warsaw, working as an apprentice for an electrical company. He was married too, but they had only one child. The oldest of the sisters, Martha, who was in her second year at the University, studied economics. Elizabeth and Mary were still at home, with me. Joshua, the youngest brother, helped our father on the farm. Our family lived and worked the farm as long as we possibly could before World War II came.

The invasion of Poland exploded into our country on September the first,1939, at 4:45 am. One and a half million German soldiers invaded Poland along its 1,750 miles on all of its western, northwestern, and southwestern borders. By September the eighth of the same year, the Nazi forces reached the outskirts of Warsaw. Germany had advanced 140 miles in the first week of the invasion. In order to stop the USSR from coming to the aid of Poland, Germany signed a non-aggression pact with Russia and secretly promised to divide the spoils equally.

To make matters worse, the Russians claimed they were helping the Poles, but they were in the war expecting to gain everything they could. Unknowingly, the Poles gave the USSR soldiers a clear run through our country, believing Russian aid was going to the Polish forces fighting the Germans on the western side. All the while, the USSR forces attacked Poland from the Eastern border. When Hitler saw his troops advancing with little or no problems, he surprisingly attacked the USSR and seized all of Poland for Germany.

Every night, I heard the sirens warning us of the incoming airplanes that dropped the bombs. During the day, I remember seeing the German and Russian soldiers pillaging everything. Women and girls were raped and sometimes even killed. Whatever was not destroyed by them, or laid claim to, was worthless to all of us. So many atrocities were committed, and nothing could be done to stop them. I remember the German soldiers coming in and killing every kind of animal. The garden produce was taken from our hands, and what the Nazis couldn't take they burned or destroyed. The wheat that needed harvesting was torched into flames.

I do remember that some of the Russian officers were nice, though. They gave us kids candy in exchange for gathering up all the food we could find. They offered to pay us to catch the pigs and the chickens, and we did, but they lied and never paid us anything. We realized their lies and false offers too late. The soldiers didn't want to get dirty or sweaty doing what we did for them. I still remember the complete devastation done to our home and our country.

After the Nazi forces left the countryside, leaving us with nothing, we went hungry, sometimes for days. I know you're sitting there thinking, "Poor little old Eleanor." You may even be thinking…should I ask her… "Do you think you guys were the only ones who lost everything?"

I know we were not. But I'm telling you what happened to me, relating what we went through, recounting my experiences, and how I felt during the time I was growing up in Poland.

We suffered hunger pangs like you can't imagine, especially after my father died. Shortly after that, both John and James were drafted into the army, and both died in the war. From then on, Mother took anything of value and sold it to buy food. She worked day and night until we were able to escape out of Poland and embark to the United States of America. By that time, Elizabeth had also died. As we were fleeing from Poland, Martha got sick and became so weak that when the doctor came to the place we were hiding, he told my mother there was nothing he could do for our sister. She died, and we all cried, except Mom. I never saw her shed a tear. Now, looking back, I don't think she could cry. I don't think she had anything left inside her to lose, not even a single tear. After we buried Martha, somewhere in the countryside, we continued our journey.

I remember coming into a small town sometime after dark. We spent the night there in a barn. The straw smelled of urine and of dung where the cows had stood while being milked, but only the smells remained because there were no animals left in our country. We ate what we could find. Sometimes we had a real treat; rotten potatoes that we found and thanked God for, because at other times we didn't have anything to put into our stomachs.

One day as our family was traveling through the countryside, we stopped for the night and hid in a grain bin. The next morning the farmer found us there. Instead of running us off, he told my youngest brother Joshua that if he helped him for the day, he would allow us to have some of the oats stored in the granary. The task at hand was to rid as many birds from the granary as possible, so that they didn't eat and defecate on so much of the grain. Mom said that if we all did the work together, it would be easier, and faster. She suggested that we catch as many of the birds as we could, by placing a gunny sack over the one window found in the granary. Joshua did just that. We helped out by waving other old sacks around, guiding the sparrows into the only opening where the gunny sack was.

Our efforts produced a catch of seventy sparrows, and that evening Mother fixed us a delicious soup. We had the best meal we'd been served for months. I don't remember how she did it, but I do remember eating. It filled our stomachs to the point that we felt like we were rich; wealthier than when we all still lived and worked on our farm as an entire family. I felt like a princess living in a fairyland kingdom, having attended a fancy banquet. We ate the entire soup without leaving even a drop of the broth to dry in the bottom of the pot.

To this day, I haven't eaten anything that's tasted so delicious as that sparrow soup. That meal of seventy sparrows was fit for a queen!

A Kind of Seraphim
by Morgan Callan Rogers

I was taking a night stroll in autumn, kicking leaves aside,
when suddenly, a gentle force drew me into itself and
I was wrapped in a circle of grace; in sweet grass and light.
Seven angels spun me round; blessed me seven times.
I cried out in absolute joy as I shed the weight of my body.
I reached out to touch their alabaster silver wings, as
they began to whisper secrets of the universe to me.
They pressed their light, perfumed bodies against me, crowd-
ing my heart as I writhed in fire spreading holy heat.
And just before I understood all that had been hidden to me
they cried out in seven tongues, and took off into the sky,
vanishing into the core of the blue night like sacred smoke.
They left me here. Adrift. Staring up at endless galaxies,
hearing only the stir of dry, dead leaves in a fall apple tree.
I knew they would not be back. Had they been here at all?
I put my hands into my pockets because they were cold.
There I found two feathers, each as warm as heaven.

Grace
by James Bowers

In my nightmare, shadows deepen. The undergrowth of doubt and helplessness tear at the throbbing ganglion of nerves in the dark forest of my soul. Asleep, there is no hope, nothing that can be done. The trees coalesce into rigid walls. The threatening sky, the fertile earth, are hard, impervious. The walls diminish until they become a concrete grave, the wooden coffin—a last, final protection against the decay of that spark of light we call life.

Buried, I still live a death in life, meaningless, beyond human control. In that grave life of motionless limbs, I have no choice but to cry out soundlessly. My only hope is in the glimmer of light. In it is power, strength to do what I cannot do myself.

I awaken horrified, only to fall again into a black hole. I descend a spiral staircase of turreted granite without windows. At the bottom, a massive wooden door will not open. Suddenly, I am inside a room where groups of persons engage in lively conversation, all strangers yet strangely familiar. I find myself drawn into a cluster of hideous personages, fearsome to behold despite the pleasant sound of their speech. I cannot understand a word of what they are saying. At first, I remain silent, aloof, refusing to join in their laughter, determined to have nothing to do with them. Then I am part of the group, laughing and crying, listening, and sympathizing, until I merge with each one, and we become a single, ethereal body. Instead of fear I feel warmth, joy, even ecstasy.

The unforgettable dream occurred over fifty years ago. The joy remains. The despair I had felt has long since disappeared. I had done nothing, only dreamed, yet somehow a transformation took place. I emerged from the forest into sunlight, drawn outside myself into a bliss of reverence by the rose-fingered rays of the sun. For the first time, I could see the beauty of a single, red rose in a slender vase on my bedside table.

The stifling grave has become a many-storied mansion which I roam in meditation and in dreams, listening to delightful conversation among the personages of my soul. Now I not only hear but also understand the voices within. I encourage them to speak for themselves on blank pages of a book I am writing. And so they do. Standing aside, I smile as each story unfolds of its own accord and wait patiently to discover what the ending will be.

PART FIVE

Illusion of Control

Fade
by Kathy Bjornestad

"Hello. I'm Zeb. Who are you?"

"Crimson."

"Huh?"

"Crimson. Like the color. Like the maples in fall. Crimson . . . like blood."

That's how we met, Zeb and me. On the bus. Both of us headed for second grade. His was the almost last stop out in Blackwater Estates, a fancy name for ten-acre tracts of wooded property with no covenants, filled with a mishmash of survivalists, retirees, retro-hippies, and regular people. Zeb's family fell into the last category. And mine? Hmmm, now that's a question.

I was last stop on a rutted road that meandered along the creek. Our land wasn't technically even part of the Estates, and I'd no idea how many acres enclosed the brambles, bracken, and sinister, hump-backed trees that thrived in its shady confines. Once there was a rock wall along our borders, but time and weather had cracked mortar and tumbled stone. In places, vines and thorn bushes shrouded the old wall, and in others, natural gateways had opened, so that the wall kept nothing in or out.

As far as I knew.

That first day of second grade in a strange place, Zeb became my only friend. Right away I took to him. The bus smelled like moldy socks and old salami, but Zeb smelled like Ivory soap and fabric softener. I leaned closer and breathed him in, then backed away so I could get a good look.

106

He was odd, that boy. To see his flattish nose, wide lips, and kinky hair, you'd think him African American, but those locks held the gloss of burnished aspen leaves, and those green eyes, the luster of a northern spring.

I found him beautiful.

And I wondered what he thought of me, with my raggedy brunette braids, eyes so dark blue they were almost black, pale skin, and cheeks that reddened whenever I got mad, or sad, or embarrassed . . . or lied like I was doing right now, as I told Zeb, "I just moved here from Florida. My parents died in a plane wreck, and the judge sent me up here to live with my aunts."

Zeb's head tipped to one side. He studied me. "You don't look like you're from Florida. Didn't you go outside?"

I felt my cheeks flush even more. "I don't like the sun. I like to read."

His green eyes lit up like Christmas lights. "Me, too! I've read all the *Kingdom of Fantasy's*, and I want to start the Harry Potters, but Mom says they're too long." As an afterthought, he added, "Sorry about your parents."

I wasn't. Not really. Mostly because I couldn't remember them. My life up till a few months ago was a blank. No memories, no stories, no loving arms or gentle scolds or bedtime stories. Just a black hole that might suck me down if I dreamed too deeply or questioned too much.

Something had filled my seven years of life, but Auntie Pearl and Auntie Em (short for Emerald, she said) clammed up when I asked. They'd just look at me with those identical black eyes staring out of impossibly large, round faces. Their meaty hands would twist each other like dishrags, and one or the other would say, "If you can't remember, that's your brain protecting your heart. When the time is right, it'll come back to you." And then they'd fade away from my bedside, murmuring to each other in rusty voices.

I understood that they weren't human. They were seven feet tall, with legs like tree trunks and mottled, gray-green skin. I'd studied my own skin, then looked at myself in the mirror that hung from my bedroom door. A month after I'd arrived, I'd cornered Auntie Em in the kitchen, where she was sorting mushrooms into piles by color and size. She wore a sack-like dress of woven mosses and a bear-tooth necklace about her thick neck.

"Auntie Em, what are you?"

She jumped at my voice and knocked a pile of spotty gray mushrooms across the table. "Wh . . . what?"

"What are you?"

"I's your aunt, child."

"No, you're not. You don't look like me."

"You take after the other side of the family." Her eyes slid away from mine.

"The human side?"

"Yes, the . . ." She realized the slip and compressed her lips.

"Are you ogres? Trolls?" I had just finished reading a Grimm's Fairy Tale book I'd found in my bookcase.

Just then Auntie Pearl appeared in the doorway. She was a little shorter and thinner than Auntie Em, but the same stringy black hair fell from her head, scalp showing through. "No such thing! We's fey, sister and I. But not black fey."

"Hmmm." I frowned. "But what am I?"

Auntie Pearl frowned at Auntie Em. "Well, you's mostly human. Enough to pass."

I digested this. "How do you pass? You know. To get food and stuff?"

Auntie Em explained, "We used to turn invisible, but now we's getting old, and it's so much easier to shop Amazon Prime. They deliver to the mailbox, and we sneak down at night and collect the goods."

"Invisible!" I exclaimed, at the same time Auntie Pearl hissed, "Too much information, Em!"

"Can I turn invisible?"

They looked at each other. "No?" they said uncertainly.

"How do you do it?" I looked to Auntie Em, who seemed more forthcoming than Auntie Pearl.

"Why, you just hold yer breath," she croaked. She sucked in air, then pressed her lips closed. Her face took on a purple tinge, and her edges blurred. She seemed to shrink.

"Cool!"

Auntie Em expelled her breath and solidified once more. Auntie Pearl tsked.

"What? It didn't scare her, did it?" Auntie Em held her hands out, palms up.

Auntie Pearl just snorted.

"But what about my parents? The kids at school all have them."

"We's your parents now, child," Auntie Em soothed. She patted me on the head with her fat-knuckled paw, like I was a dog. "And it might be best if you don't stick out. So can you pretend invisibility when you's away from us, child? Fer yer own good?"

Auntie Pearl moved into the kitchen and pulled a platter wrapped in tinfoil from the refrigerator. She set it on the counter and peeled back the covering to reveal leftover meatloaf and a huddle of baked potatoes. The aunts were both vegetarians, but they'd been trying hard, for my sake. She heaped a plate and set it on the table. Auntie Em selected two slick black mushrooms and three plump white ones from her piles. She plopped them in a wooden bowl and joined me at the table.

"Why can't I remember, Auntie Em?" I complained. My lower lip trembled.

"Hush, now." Auntie Pearl filled her own bowl, poured three glasses of goat's milk, brought them to us, and sat down with her mushrooms. The milk tasted funny, but I drank it. They were trying so hard.

I swallowed back tears. "You have to know something. You have to."

Auntie Pearl pulled at her stringy hair. She looked to Auntie Em, who was kneading her arms and squinching up her nose. Together they said, "We don't."

Then Auntie Pearl sighed and said, "They brought you here to us eight weeks ago. No markings on you. No note. You was

110

passed out, and didn't wake up till the next morning. They told us nothing. Never do."

"Except her name, Sister," Auntie Em chimed in. "They did tell her name."

"Crimson. Nothing more."

"Who is they? And how did I get a last name then?"

At the same time, one said, "The fey royal guard," and the other said, "We made one up."

I looked from one to the other. "You made up Rue? Why?"

"Because it means regret, child," said Auntie Pearl.

Auntie Em added quickly, "And we's figured your real parents must've had a lot of regret about losing you. Right, Pearl?"

"That's right."

My eyes welled up. I was so sensitive back then. "Maybe Rue is a bad name. Maybe my parents wanted to get rid of me."

"No, no," they repeated over and over and plied me with cookies that tasted of maple and bark. They petted me and read me stories and offered me a pet snail. Later, in my bed, alone, I lay on my back and looked out the window at the round, pale moon. And I had another thought. If the aunts were right, and my parents had loved me, what must they be feeling now?

Somehow that was even worse than imagining I had been unwanted.

***

Time passed. I quit hoping my memory would return. I grew from a petite grade-schooler into a gangly seventh grader, and Zeb grew right along with me, only he somehow managed to do it more gracefully. His limbs stayed in proportion, and though his face's baby roundness diminished, he remained essentially unchanged.

That year, a new boy moved into Blackwater Estates. His fancy name—Pascal Reeves—matched his fancy designer shirts. When the winter sun hit the many fancy windows in his fancy house, the place seemed to burn like a giant star exploding. At first Zeb and I yearned to know him. Our school was small and rural. New kids were rare, exotic animals whose favor must be curried.

So, on the bus ride home a week after he'd arrived, while we waited for other kids to disembark, Zeb approached the new boy. "Hey there," he said. "I'm Zeb," just like he'd introduced himself to me all those years ago.

Reeves looked up (nobody called him "Pascal"). He'd been scowling out the window. Now he turned that scowl on my friend. "So?"

That single syllable, uttered beneath heavy-lidded eyes, matched a careless slouch that proclaimed he couldn't care less about us. My fingernails bit into my palms. I scooted to the edge of the seat, ready to defend Zeb, who only blinked and replied, "So you look like you could use a friend."

Reeves stood up. He was taller than Zeb, and solid in a way Zeb, with his willow-tree limbs, wasn't. Dark hair fell across a broad forehead. Hazel eyes regarded Zeb coolly. "You saying I look pathetic, sitting up here all alone? That it?"

Zeb repeated with gentle patience, "You look like you could use a friend."

Reeves' fist swung back and shot forward, right into Zeb's stomach. A huff of air whooshed from Zeb's lungs. He folded like a pocketknife.

It took me two seconds to process this unfathomable attack. Then I was on that new kid, my mind a red buzz of outrage. Something raw and mean and possibly magical uncurled inside me. Heat burned into my fingertips. I clawed at Reeves' face and snarled like a wildcat. I kicked his shins with my leather-toed shoes. When he grabbed my wrists and held me off, I spat in his face.

The magic felt ready to burst out of my skin, but I remembered the aunts and held back. Beside me, Zeb had caught his breath and stumbled to his feet. Up front, the bus driver, Connie, was yelling, "Hey!" and trying to untangle herself from the gearshift. Behind Zeb and me, a background of titters told me the other kids were enjoying the show. I didn't care. Not yet, anyway. The mindless anger still controlled me, and it felt really good—like a monster crouched inside had broken free.

Zeb grabbed me around the waist and hauled me away from Reeves, who wiped spittle off his cheek. Connie got up in my face and blustered something about calling my parents and referring me to the office. Big deal. The rush of violence had faded, leaving me shaky. I slumped against Zeb, who pulled me back into our seat. Reeves smirked and turned away from us.

Connie stalked off and returned a moment later with a yellow slip of paper. She made me sign it and held up a hand when Zeb tried to explain that Reeves had started the fight. I clutched Zeb and whispered, "Doesn't matter." Connie frumped off to her seat, and the bus inched from the curb with a pneumatic hiss.

We regarded Reeves' dark head two seats in front of us, then each other. "You all right?" I asked Zeb.

He nodded, green eyes like shards of sea glass holding mine.

"You didn't need to jump on him like that, but thanks." Zeb paused. He picked up the sketchbook he often drew in during the long bus ride and ruffled the pages. He bit his lip.

"What?"

"You were really mad. Like you could've killed him."

I considered this. The rage had flashed like an electrical storm, effortless and exhilarating. "Maybe I could've. I don't know. Sometimes I feel invisible, you know? But when I hit him, I felt solid . . . like concrete." I relished the memory. "Do you ever feel invisible?"

"Invisible is what other people see or don't see. Guess I never cared enough about their opinions to feel anything either way. Not that I don't like people. I just don't need them. Except you. I think I might need you, Crimson."

My cheeks heated. "Well, we're friends. We shouldn't be invisible to each other. But doesn't it matter that Reeves hit you?"

"It just answers the question, 'Can we be friends?' with an exclamation point, that's all." He laughed.

I thought of the aunts, and how they sometimes turned invisible for me, and how I'd thought it was the coolest thing. "You don't care about standing out or hiding, either one, do you? That's kind of amazing, Zeb."

"In a good or bad way?" A frown creased his forehead, like he really cared what I thought.

I punched his arm. "Good, of course."

"I hope you don't get kicked off the bus, Crimson. How would we really see each other except at lunch?"

The aunts wouldn't let me visit Zeb's house, nor was he allowed to come over, for obvious reasons. (They said their fey looks would be too hard for Zeb's human brain to process.) I didn't really believe them, but I did believe some things. Like the aunts would have magicked me invisible to protect me if they could have.

So I kept practicing in my room late at night. I held my breath, visualized, willed my edges to fade. But apparently the fey part of me (if there was one) was too weak to perform that sort of magic.

There are many ways to become invisible, though. I'd mastered some of them pretty well until the bus incident. I never raised my hand, never volunteered for anything, never did too well or too poorly on assignments. I wore jeans and t-shirts without logos. I avoided sports, plays, music, and any other activities that might draw attention to myself. Sometimes when I looked in the mirror, I wondered who that girl was staring back at me. I was easy to forget.

***

The next day on the bus, Zeb scooted over to make room for me and said, "So the principal didn't kick you off. I was worried."

I sat down, backpack in my lap. "No, just a warning. Don't worry. He'll forget all about me before long. I'm good at giving people amnesia."

"I don't think Reeves will ever forget you."

"That's not good. The aunts wouldn't like that." I frowned.

"Forget the aunts. It is good."

I raised my eyebrows at him.

Zeb drew a deep breath. "Crimson, you're always talking about your aunts making you keep a low profile, but I've been thinking it's not healthy. Taking risks can be a good thing. I mean, I'm not known as a risk-taker, but I say what I think, and I express myself. See?" He held up his sketchbook, and there was me—a weird me, dressed in a hooded cloak, timid as Little Red Riding Hood facing the wolf in Grandma's bed.

"Is that how you see me?"

"No. This is how I see you." Zeb flipped a page and brought up another sketch of me in a Wonder Girl outfit, eyes uplifted, one fist raised to strike.

I giggled. "I like that one better."

"Me, too, so be her. I'd be your friend either way, but you'll like yourself more this way." He jabbed at the superhero girl.

"Maybe it's too dangerous. The aunts—"

"I said forget them! You need to be happy, Crimson. Ever since I've known you, you've been hiding something. And see what happens? Eventually, everything spills out anyway."

"In a scary way."

"Yeah, and it might've felt good for a minute, and you might've been protecting me, but it was out of control. You freaked me out a little."

"Sorry."

"So?"

"I don't know. I'll think about it." I leaned my elbows on my navy-blue backpack. I considered my missing past, and the aunts, and the weird but kind of delightful way we lived in the woods. I thought about my best friend Zeb and how I could have more friends if I put myself out there. I thought about all the things I'd missed, the things I secretly wanted to try, and how being invisible wasn't all it was cracked up to be.

I stood up.

The bus was moving. We weren't supposed to stand.

Ignoring Zeb's protestations, I slid from my seat and walked over to Reeves. He looked up, scorn and fear fighting for expression.

"I'm sorry I kicked and scratched you," I said. "You probably have bigger problems at home than I do, and you were just taking out your own insecurities on Zeb."

"Go away, loser."

The magic inside me stirred. I pondered his response, then replied, "No, I don't think so. I've been trying to go away my whole life. And I'm not happy. I really think the secret to happiness might be sticking around for all the joy and pain, not trying to make myself vanish. That emotional stuff comes out anyway. You can't avoid it by blurring the edges."

A muscle ticked in Reeves' cheek. "You're psycho."

A flicker of heat raced down my fingers. I willed my magic to stay. I shrugged. "Name-calling doesn't bother me. That's just what bullies do. But it will bother me if you attack my friend again, so don't even think about it. I've got superpowers you haven't seen yet."

Reeves shifted in his seat. "Whatever. Can you just go away now?" His eyes shifted to Connie, and I wondered if he'd actually gotten in trouble, too, when I'd explained to Principal Alan that I'd been defending Zeb.

I felt good. Not the wild-rush good that totally losing control had given me, but a sort of steady, level-headed good. "Sure," I nodded agreeably and returned to my seat.

Zeb heaved a sigh of relief. "I thought you were going to slug him again."

"Why would I do that?" I raised an eyebrow.

Zeb just smiled and tapped the drawing of me as Wonder Girl.

I told him, "You know, musical tryouts are next week, and I think I'd make a good lead."

Zeb's smile broadened. "You might not get it," he warned.

"That's okay. Trying is what counts."

Hail Anem
by Jean Helmer

An anem is three poems in one. Each horizontal line has ten syllables. The first poem is found reading left to right. A second poem is found by reading only the left side from the top down. Poem three is found by reading the right side from the bottom to the top. "Anem" means "two fountains." The poem's physical layout reveals the fountains.

Hail	pea-sized pellets' proclamation: doom
Clear, flat domes	frozen sky tortoises join
Medieval maces	bare jagged ice fangs
Nature's wrath unleashed, ruthless	destruction
Man's illusion of control vanquished	storm

Arizona Storm
by Holly Moseley

The monsoons are upon us,
the desert is all abloom
after the hovering clouds
remove their cover of gloom.

But again the rain is coming,
gentle, then fast and strong;
a steady thrumming on the roof,
sets the beat to its song.

The lightning moves ever closer,
the thunder comes quick and loud,
rain pounds down upon us
from an all-encompassing cloud.

A snap, a pop, I jump!
And the dog runs under my chair:
then–the smell of lightning,
sharp in the clean-washed air.

Now the day is brightening,
the thunder rumbles by;
rain sounds a pitter-patter,
clouds scud across the sky.

The storm, as it passes beyond us
becomes a steady, lulling shower.
But the lingering touch of lightning remains,
an acrid aroma of power.

The Legend of Old Blue
by Dawn Newland

Jim Thornhill stood admiring how the red granite walls began to darken against the still turquoise sky above. A hint of sunlight rimmed the opposite side of the Salt River Cañon and lay a golden path downward following the tops of every rock escarpment. The purple shadows of evening were marching up from the bottom, one outcropping to the next. "Like the grand staircase to heaven," Jim said to himself.

He had ridden the flaxen-maned sorrel he called Seven Up, and led Monte, the stout, black-footed bay. The pair were the best tie-down rope horses a man could hope to have, sure-footed in the rocks and savvy about handling big, wild cattle. The old ponies were inseparable, and he could let them out to graze at night with no worries of them quitting camp.

The mule he packed along wasn't so loyal. Jim called him Hammer, short for Hammer Head. Hammer was as cantankerous as he was tough. After unpacking, Jim hobbled him.

The high and treacherous red rock walls of the cañon were broken up on either side by sheer cuts and washes that tied dry creek beds to the twisted river below. The channels ran big water when it rained. It hadn't rained in a long while. Cattle sign had been plentiful all day, with tracks leading down the dry washes. Close to the river, the air was pungent with the smells of disturbed brush and fresh manure. Jim camped in the tree line just up from the only obvious watering spot.

His boy, Bill, had quit him again for a weekend of girlin' in town. Bill had made him promise not to be roping any of the big steers alone.

Most of the easy-to-handle critters had been shipped or thrown back out of the rough country. All that remained along this confluence were the big old revolutionaries. They knew the dim trails and hideaways up from the river. Their game was laying low … brushing up, then going on the prod if jumped or cornered.

They'd worked the country back of Haystack Butte all last week. It was closer to the regular cow camp and the holding pasture. Generally, the big wild cattle would require a bit of education before lining out. He or Bill would end up busting the renegades two or three times to get them civilized enough to trail with a gentler bunch. One old mossy-horned mutineer they'd left tied to a tree for two days until they could find a gentler one to pair him with. Bill had commented that day, "Christ, he must be old enough to vote."

As Jim crawled into his bed tarp, he made up his mind to do nothing more than scout for a couple days until Bill found him again. When morning came, Hammer was in a fine mess and Jim had to untangle him from the picket line before graining him. The geldings had nickered at the first sound of him stirring. He slipped their nosebags on and sat back for his first cup of coffee.

The mule's head jerked up, and his big ears twitched forward. Hammer stared intently over his nosebag and let out a muffled snort. Jim scanned the dimly lit clearing knowing Hammer was like having a good watchdog. He squatted to wait, quietly watching the mule's ears.

Just as Jim strained the last of his coffee through his teeth, an old, ring-horned blue roan steer stepped tentatively into the clearing, not three hundred yards below his well-hidden camp. The blue stood to attention, nerves twitching his skin, as he sniffed the air like only wild cattle do. Jim knew the blue by reputation only. The morning breeze was in Jim's favor. He sat tight and hoped the mule would keep quiet.

These kinds always sneaked into the water holes early. Jim was wise to their habits. If left alone, the roan would tank up and then graze his way back to the rim. By midday he'd be shaded up fighting flies, lost to a brush thicket.

The minute the blue critter dropped out of sight down to the river, Jim stood to remove the feedbags from his horses and the mule. Having seen the size of the animal, he bridled the bay horse. Monte was at least two hundred pounds heavier than Seven Up, not as fast but brush smart and sure-footed; most importantly, he could hold back a freight train on a mountain slope.

The legend of the blue steer had been passed around evening campfires for years. Tall tales of him chasing men off the mountain had become so numerous and far-fetched that no one even believed he was still alive, or maybe he never had been. Seemed every fall some lone cowhand would spot him, but always from a mile away. His size and fame had grown with each passing year.

The first time Jim realized Blue might be more than thin air and tall tales was when the whiskey came out at the shipping yards last fall. George Cline was oiled pretty good. At the boys' urging, he got to retelling his encounter with Old Blue. George laughed and swore that Blue's eyes were made of fire and his horns of shiny black marble. He claimed to have seen the devil steer honing them on the sycamore trees, and that's why they were sharp as sabers and white at the tips.

Jim knew George well enough to know there was more than a little truth behind the entertaining yarn he spun. According to legend, the blue monster had never been caught. George had said any good cowboy would have remembered his odd coloring and the unique white heart in the middle of his broad blue forehead. But he sure had been caught, at least once, for he was branded with a running squiggle of a scar on his left hip and both ears were undercut. George's theory was that his wild mama had hid him out along Cherry Creek until he was a slick two-year-old bull. He figured that rustlers had made a run at him. They'd only gotten him half-branded and half-castrated when Blue had escaped and went on the rampage. "Probably, there's a cold fire and old running irons scattered somewhere in a wash," George had laughed. "Blue's been purely hateful toward mankind ever since."

The critter sure enough had the look of a stag. Jim stood still and watched, while mulling the urge to give the blue phantom a run. "If Lady Luck rides with me, I'd get one good throw at the devil," he muttered.

In less than a heartbeat, Jim was saddled and leading Monte silently out of camp. Once, he heard the mule whiffle a snort behind him, and then all was still. He tightened the cinch and mounted to circle above the trail the steer had come down on. Monte moved like a cat as they ghosted up the sidehill. Jim checked his extra catch rope and loosened his soft, braided tie-down ropes he kept looped through his chap belt at his waist. He seated his old Merwin revolver deep in his waistband with the same motion.

There'd be one chance at the blue steer, and he intended on taking it. His loop was built. Monte's ears snapped forward and back. The skin along the bay's neck trembled with knowing they were on the hunt and would soon be jumping a wild critter. Monte loved the chase.

It never failed to surprise Jim that his own nerves twitched at the prospect of a wild run. His plan was to wait until the steer came to him. He'd jump him out and head him back down the hill. He figured to be close enough before being spotted to catch the roan just as he broke into the clearing. The steer would gain the advantage if he reached the heavy timbered area across the clearing or took to the river.

To Jim, having a plan was key; of equal importance was knowing when to throw the plan to the wind. There were rarely any rules of order when working wild cattle.

124

Jim waited what seemed an hour before he heard Blue coming. The steer poked along, ambling up the trail, heavy gutted with his fill of water. Jim figured he'd be too full to make much of a run. It was a split-second decision to not wait for Blue's move. His hope was that he could haze the renegade to the holding pasture. Maybe find some gentler white faces to use as bait along the way. Jim had his loop ready and tucked under his arm to keep it from catching on the trees he was crashing under and over.

Blue proved to be a sprinter, even full of water. Jim circled him in the clearing and spurred Monte up to make one long reaching throw. He missed. Monte was still fresh. "How do we feel about Blue now?" Jim talked as he coiled his rope. "Well, Pard, we better at least give him another run for his money." Sounds of the steer crashing timber came from off to the right and up the mountain from him. "The rascal," Jim muttered, "he's being foolish in tryin' to get back to his stompin' grounds." Jim smiled to himself and hit a trot up the sidehill. They tracked Blue like a lion tracks a deer. Up and down the slope, they weaved for an hour.

Monte's step was still eager, and his ears were working back and forth with a watchfulness as Jim urged him in pursuit. Suddenly, there came a mighty hullabaloo from behind an out-cropping of boulders. It sounded like a hundred head of cattle had hit the brush ahead of them. Then it became quiet. Monte's step and his labored breathing were too loud. Jim brought him to a standstill and studied the ground for tracks. He could make out the disturbed rocks, bent grass stems, and the broken branches where Blue had veered off the main trail. Jim was met with a horde of buzzing flies. He cautiously approached what appeared to be a brushy, frequently used hideout behind a large, house-sized boulder.

Jim bent forward to squint under the low-hanging mesquite trees growing out of the base of the rocks. There before him stood the legend of Old Blue with two fireballs blazing where he should have had eyes. He'd whirled to make his stand. The impressive horns were sure enough black as marble, except for the tips; and they were polished ivory and pointed too, just like George had described them. His big head was rocking menacingly back and forth with the tips of those monster horns clearing branches at each sweep. His tongue lolled out a foot. A wave of slobbers stringing from either side of his mouth hung on the brush like spiderwebs. What was most daunting was the roar he was releasing with every heaving breath. It wasn't a normal kind of bovine beller.

Jim drew Monte back a step and as he did, he broke a branch off and gave it a fling at the distinct white heart in the middle of the blue critter's face. "You piece of roan rawhide," Jim drawled but he never finished his thought, for Blue was done tolerating the insults. He reared up like a stud horse coming to battle. The brush cracked as he exited his hideaway to wage war. Monte spun and lunged down the trail with the steer hooking and bellowing on his tail. Jim touched the bay with a spur and realized he was giving his all. He then turned in the saddle to lay a perfect, raggedy old loop all the way over the six-foot span of horns. It settled deep around Blue's neck. Jim could see it went too deep to throw a trip.

Up close, Blue was every bit of what George had described him as, only bigger. He was closing in for the kill, and Monte wasn't going to outrun him. Jim reined the bay horse hard to the left just as Blue swung a white-tipped horn and slit his chap halfway up his leg.

Then the steer dropped back a step and ran his big head in between the horse's hind legs. That's when he went to lifting rather than hooking. Monte kicked with both hind feet, but the steer's force lifted his hindquarters to the sky; his forelegs buckled. Jim hit the ground on his hands and knees. It felt like he'd flown forty feet, but there was still the hot breath of Old Blue on his collar. Jim rolled to one side as feet and horns blew past. He scrambled again to get clear. Out of the corner of his eye, he saw Monte struggling to his feet, still attached to the monster.

Things went black for a spell; the next thing Jim knew, he was spitting blood and desperately scrambling to regain his feet. All he could think was to keep moving, for the blue devil steer was sure to come a hookin' again. Jim felt for his gun. It was gone.

Still dazed, Jim pulled himself toward a rock outcropping. When he dared a look around, a low whistle of relief was all he could manage. His old pony had somehow dragged the steer around a mesquite tree and stood leaning into the rope. It looked like the steer was choked down, maybe dead. Monte had come through for him again.

Jim stumbled around until he found his gun. As his senses began to sharpen, he looked himself over. Only a small amount of blood leaked out the top of his boot where his chaps were laid open. He was sure scuffed up but otherwise in one piece. Easing up to his horse, he spoke in an unsteady voice, "Whoa, Pard … you sure saved my bacon. Darned if you aren't a good one." Laying a hand to the bay's damp, trembling neck, Jim leaned cautiously to look at the blue monster lying in a heap at the end of his rope, "Reckon we got him."

A long, distressed groan came from deep within the water-laden steer. Jim approached with his old Merwin in one hand and his knife in the other. The steer's crown was caked with red dirt, blood oozed from his nostrils, but his horns were still intact. Jim stepped gingerly around the beast and reached for his tail. "For posterity's sake," he muttered, and cut the dung encrusted, blue and white tail switch off right below the bone. "They'll never believe me if I go home empty-handed." Jim folded the prize and stuffed it in his pocket.

As he walked around the animal, one big eye opened from Blue's matted face and blinked slowly at Jim. The fire was

gone from it. The conqueror stood staring down at the con-
quered: the prostrate body of old Blue, the notorious outlaw
of Cherry Creek; the baddest of the bad, the legend. He had
been a magnificent specimen—a true picture of survival of the
fittest. A deep sadness washed over Jim at being the one to
take that from him.

Blue was gurgling for air. There was no fight left.

"Ease up, step on up, Monte," Jim coaxed with a sudden and
overpowering urgency. Monte moved cautiously up the rope.
No slack came to the steer. "You're too damned tangled up,"
Jim talked quietly to the dying animal. "Don't be giving up the
ghost on me, old pard." There was no time to analyze what
had come over him. He still held his knife. "This one's for you,
Kid," Jim said and leaned over the roan's withers to cut the
noose from his neck.

Blue's eyes were rolled back in his head now. There came a
death shudder at the release of the rope, and his head sank
sideways to rest a black marble horn on the earth; the other
white-tipped trophy slanted skyward as he groaned again.
"Good intentions, too darned late," Jim muttered and backed
away.

He gathered his reins, led Monte a few yards down the slope.
Stray twigs and leaves filled the gullet of his saddle, and it was
jerked off-center. His hands wouldn't obey his mind. They
were bloody and swollen and still trembly. Wincing and
worming the latigo loose, Jim managed to get his rig back in
order.

Positioning Monte downslope aided the unsteady swing into
the saddle. Battered limbs protested at the strain. Jim made it
to camp and slowly went about his chores that had been interrupted at daylight. He watered both ponies and the mule in the
river below camp and rode back to pull his gear. Everything
was at a snail's pace as he rubbed Monte's sweaty hide and

legs with an old burlap grain sack. Thick and unwilling fingers made pulling mesquite and cactus thorns a slow process.

Jim uncovered his fire and stirred the coals to warm his coffee. It bothered him that the blue steer had reminded him of his old pardner, Kid Curry. He mumbled to himself, "The passing of a legend … the end of an era." That's for sure what Lucy will say. He grimaced at the thought of facing his wife. "There'll be no telling Lucy," he said and reached to rub his brow. Bewildered at finding his hat gone, he exclaimed, "Well, doggone it! Must a knocked my lights plumb out." Jim lay back and closed his eyes, searching for solid ground.

The hard midday sun had moved behind the rim and a dark, fast-moving cloud took its place. Jim groaned to his feet. He kept an eye on the building storm as he saddled Seven Up and donned his slicker before mounting.

Jim was melancholy as he turned the sorrel up the trail to where he'd left the blue steer lying under the mesquite tree. The wind had picked up and was whistling through the granite boulders along the rim above him. As much as he didn't crave seeing the old boy dead, he needed his rope. And he especially wanted his hat. If the storm hit, he'd never find it.

There was a terrible guilt plaguing him at the unfair advantage he'd taken in letting the old steer fill up on water before the run. Monte would never have stayed within a mile of Blue if he hadn't been water-laden. Jim thought about the times the Pinkertons' had pulled similar tricks on Kid—of when they'd sneaked up on little brother Loney while he ate breakfast and then justified killing him—same way he had justified catching Blue. He felt for the tail switch in his pocket and was irked at himself.

The wind was cutting slantwise in his face when he came around the outcropping of boulders. There, on the very spot Blue should have been, stood only the tattered mesquite tree.

Jim reined in, whistling out his surprise. "Well, ain't you the rascal … too darned tough to die." The relief that came over him was the same relief he'd always felt when Kid escaped some impossible trap. "By danged, you two old legends might be immortal after all." Jim laughed at the miraculous resurrection.

Jim found the hondo end of his catch rope still caught up in the tree. He glanced around just in case Blue was nearby with revenge on his mind. The only thing he saw was his hat. It was wedged in the rocks and dirt like he'd plowed a furrow with his head where Monte had first lost his footing. The rest of his rope lay a hundred yards up the trail where Blue had shaken free of it.

Like mountain storms do in Arizona, this one built and boiled in grand colors. It howled and spat empty threats, only to dissipate as he rode back to his camp. Darkness settled as he unsaddled and grained his horses. Jim spent an hour plaiting a new hondo into his rope.

Too tired to eat and too awake to sleep, Jim lay back to watch his little fire snap and hiss. Before long it danced to life and began talking of old things: days gone by, could have beens and what ifs, life and death, old friends, and legends.

One by one, stars began to fill the blue velvet sky overhead. "We was always a part of the wild things, weren't we, Kid?" Jim lamented to his old outlaw friend. He pondered the strange events of the day and wondered if Kid was in another scrape. "If so, I hope fate dealt you an ace too, ole Pard," Jim muttered, "I sure held a fist full of 'em today."

About a Doe
by Maria Lisa Eastman

Yesterday riding out on my tall horse
I came upon a doe
down behind some thick brush.
Close under her breast
she held hooves
stilled like silent castanets.
Her long ears were perfect —
colored just so,
edges brushed in black watercolor.

She gazed at me,
and I at her.
I told her I meant no harm.
I had to say something
after she tried to run.
She lunged and fell,
then again.
Each try was the half of before.
It was clear she wasn't going to run
from anything or
anyone anymore.

Now I could see
her craggy spine standing
ribs thrusting
through her haggard coat.
A line of spit from her mouth
pooled
slowly
on the dry earth.

But she looked never away.
I wondered if she really saw me
from halfway through the so-called door.
Did I blur into a tree? A fence?

Or did she see some
towering cervid Charon
waiting to take her across the river?

If I were more fanciful —
if I thought wild things
could read my heart,
I might think she understood
I was going to help.
Truly, what I felt
when I placed the muzzle
when I whispered
quiet, quiet,
and my whole body hugged the gun
was love,
edges brushed in black watercolor.

Sapphire Spring
by A.M. Hummel

A skiff of snow
glistens in the morning sun.
Wind-battered flakes whirl,
obscure blue skies,
blast as white-to-crystal powder against my window,
then push on through drifted fields.
Neighbors as winter-weary as I
share the added chill.

I fill the feeders.
Chickadees and jays and red-winged blackbirds lambast—
I've let their perceived abundance slide—
but today, the real treat is mine.
Shy, peeking from an ancient, paint-peeled birdhouse,
a plump lady bluebird,
beautiful harbinger of spring,
chirps a greeting.
Is the sweet hello directed to her sapphire mate
who sits, wind-ruffled, atop a nearby fence post,
or is the friendly trill a thank you,
and a promise
spring is near?

Summer Birds on the *Albion*
by Kathy Bjornestad

Barton first saw her on the *Albion's* quarterdeck—waif-like, but on the cusp of womanhood—wisps of russet hair escaping from beneath a wide-brimmed bonnet. Her high-waisted gown billowed like a sail in the briny wind. She might have been any English maid returning home from abroad, as displaced among tar buckets and halyards on the East India Company's merchant ship as she had been in the dirty, colorful market-places of India's Calcutta.

She shouldn't have been alone, but her companion, a pinch-faced, elderly matron, had fallen victim to seasickness the first night out and had not yet recovered. Though the girl—Lucy, her name was—appeared delicate, in truth, the man decided, she was not. Noting the way she gripped the gunwale, the straight line of her shoulders, the jut of her rather square chin, he supposed she had grown impatient of nursing Mrs. Smith and had slipped away from the closeness of their cabin when sleep took the old woman.

Miss Lucy stood firm against the rolling deck, a packet of letters clenched in her right hand. She grimaced. Her eyebrows knit. Some inner turmoil caused the hand holding the letters to clench, crumpling fragile parchment, but she didn't seem to notice. Her facial muscles twitched and lips mumbled voice-lessly in silent argument.

Barton had just decided to join her when another passenger appeared around the mizzenmast. Mr. Charles Everly, the young scientist they had picked up at Ceylon, smoothed his rumpled linen shirt (a fruitless effort, for his cravat remained askew), and slicked back windblown hair, which immediately blew up again in a brown tangle. His normally distracted-look-ing gray eyes appeared at this moment sharp as sunlight re-flected off metal. They pierced Miss Lucy like twin stars.

134

She was by no means a beautiful girl, though her position as the only female under thirty aboard the *Albion* had made the male crew and passengers tolerant of this defect. Barton had noticed several sailors casting wistful looks her way, but she paid no heed. When Mr. Everly's quiet footfalls carried him near, she turned, and a curtain descended on her inner dialogue. From his deck chair, Barton heard her exclaim, "Mr. Everly!" and saw a blush rise to her cheeks. The young man nodded, a quiet smile transforming his tanned, ordinary face into something more vibrant. Mr. Everly pointed to a gull suspended on the stiff breeze, a broad-chested fellow with sharp, avaricious eyes and a curved beak. Barton couldn't make out what conversation followed, but from Mr. Everly's gestures, it appeared he was enlightening Lucy on the mysteries of the avian species.

As a retiring missionary, Barton considered himself a fair judge of man's nature. His work had been with the soul, but understanding the intricacies of the human mind had made him successful in converting many heathens. Now he was returning to Shropshire, England, so that he might expire in the land of his birth. What else to do besides die after a life spent in far-off places filled with dark magic and tropical climes, mystical shamans and sloe-eyed women? He had thought nothing more in this life could surprise him, yet he now found himself surprised, and, yes, intrigued.

The couple retreated from the railing and sat down just past a pile of hemp rope. Pretending to read his dog-eared Bible, Barton caught snatches of their conversation.

"I have another book you might enjoy, Miss Lucy," Charles Everly was saying in a mild, hesitant tone.

"Oh, Mr. Everly?"

"Have you heard of Maria Merian?" A pause. "She was a woman scientist who studied entomology. Her work, unfortunately, is not well-read, but brilliant in its method. In a time when creatures with the ability to metamorphose were considered evil, she proved that such shape-changers were simply a fascinating part of nature."

"Do you mean butterflies, for instance?"

Mr. Everly nodded energetically. "Exactly. Summer birds, she called them. Isn't that poetic?"

"Summer birds," Miss Lucy repeated.

Barton slid a glance toward the young people and started. When he had first seen the girl, he thought her caterpillar-plain. But now, Mr. Everly's enthusiasm touched her like sunlight, transforming a stoic countenance into a lively flame. Towards the start of their journey, he had thought, this girl is similar to me, a creature on the fringes of life. But now he realized he was wrong. Like an insect tearing free of its cocoon, she glowed with life.

Barton worried his lower lip. Everly had placed a brown hand familiarly over Lucy's pale one. Mrs. Smith would not approve.

Oblivious to Barton's attention, the companions rose. Mr. Everly took Miss Lucy's arm, and they strolled off. The packet of letters lay forgotten on the deck chair. A breeze made the pages flutter like a pigeon's tail feathers, and, afraid the missives might decide to fly, he rose stiffly and scooped them up. He started after their owner, then realized she was already too far away for his arthritic legs to intercept. Barton had no mind to call out, so he tucked the letters into his coat and retired to his cabin, where he laid them atop a sea chest, untouched, while he went to dinner.

Neither Miss Lucy nor Charles Everly appeared that night, an event too coincidental to be a benign occurrence, yet the grizzled captain, along with a middle-aged couple returning to England for the birth of their first grandchild, seemed unsuspicious. Mrs. Leigh-Carlton lost no opportunity in opening the conversation with, "I see poor Miss Lucy isn't with us tonight. Is she feeling unwell?"

The captain, a red-cheeked, jowly man with tropic-blue eyes, sipped his ale, then replied, "I believe she is once again nursing the unfortunate Mrs. Smith, whom, it appears, is never to achieve her sea legs."

Mrs. Leigh-Carlton tutted, "Such a shame."

Her husband tried to intercept the conversation with, "I recall your first trip overseas, my dear, and the horrible. . ."

But his wife was not to be distracted and, with an impatient glance his way, she continued, "Such a plain little thing, Miss Lucy, and yet so polite, so unassuming. Could no other husband be discovered for her in India?"

The captain cleared his throat, clearly uncomfortable, and shrugged.

Mr. Leigh-Carlton seized the opportunity to interject and declared, "It was, of course, a small community of foreigners. And at five and twenty, Miss Lucy is no dewy maiden. Had she more fortune, she might have found another man to marry her, but as it is . . ."

Mrs. Leigh-Carlton joined him in sympathetic head-shaking.

Barton stayed silent, observing but not partaking, as was his wont. He took in the Leigh-Carltons, middle-class social climbers who possessed the manners of the bourgeoisie with their subtle, greedy crassness covered only by a thin veneer of Christian charity. He did not care for them.

Mrs. Leigh-Carlton clicked her tongue again. "But what will Miss Lucy do in England? Will relatives take her in?"

"I believe there is an older sister," the captain replied, "with an abundance of children."

"Ah, I see." A look of pity flitted over Mrs. Leigh-Carlton's face, and Barton wondered if he had misjudged her. But then she shrugged. "At least the poor girl shall be cared for. It is not a life I would have chosen, but to each her own." She slid a smug glance toward her browbeaten husband, who studied his last bite of salt pork with dubious attention.

Barton almost spoke in defense of Miss Lucy, whom he very much doubted had chosen to nursemaid her sister's children. If she had agreed to it, her aim had likely been to unburden her parents.

No one mentioned Mr. Charles Everly. He often forgot to attend dinner in favor of writing in his scientific journal. What conversation he possessed did not seem to suit the Leigh-Carltons or the captain, for neither shared his passion for academic pursuits. Barton had spoken to Mr. Everly a time or two, however, and found him to be an engaging fellow if one knew how to listen—a man of books, not of the world. Yet the world seemed to fascinate him much as it did Barton, as something to be observed for its small miracles and surprising patterns. How lucky I have been, thought he, to have seen so much of it. But now all that is over.

Shaking off a sudden melancholy, Barton excused himself and retreated to his cabin. Just before he reached it, a slight form materialized out of the dimness below decks. Miss Lucy. He stopped her as she edged around him in the narrow passageway and said, "Pardon me, Miss, but you left your letters in a

138

deck chair, and I have them in my cabin. I can fetch them for you."

Her eyebrows rose like wings, and color stained her cheeks. She seemed distracted, and it took a moment for her green eyes to focus on him. "Oh," she said, twisting her hands together. "You needn't have bothered, really. I'm finished with them. In fact . . ." a violent trembling took hold of her voice, "throw them overboard, please. Or do anything with them. I care not. I shan't want them back."

He hadn't thought he could be shocked anymore, but this reply held him speechless. Letters were a precious commodity to be treasured and reread. He stuttered, "As you wish, Miss," then started to add more, but she had already curtsied and turned away.

The packet, tied with blue ribbon, had slipped from the chest onto the floor. He picked it up, lit a kerosene lamp, and sat down stiffly on his narrow bunk. Barton stared at the bundle. Throw them overboard. He repeated her words to himself. Yet he was curious. Why did the letters mean so little to her? He chided himself for being just such a busybody as Mrs. Leigh-Carlton, yet his thick-knuckled fingers fumbled with the ribbon, and it fell away.

Dearest Lucy,

I have just received your latest letter, and I must scold you for being neglectful. Does Calcutta society keep you so busy that you cannot take time for your poor sister, tucked into the boring countryside whilst you dance and socialize your way through a foreign and exotic locale? But do not pity me, dear sister, for tomorrow we dine at the Ashcrofts. Anna will attend, as will John Butler. You recall how we played together as children? He is much changed since the war, and walks with a heavy limp. I thought at one time he might do for you, but as he is now engaged to Clara Jones, I must rely on Father to find you a suitable husband...

Barton stopped reading and frowned. The lamp's flame danced wickedly behind its smoke-blackened pane. He tossed the first letter on the coverlet and picked up a second.

Oh Dear Lucy,

I just received word from Father of your engagement! Please forgive any attempts at matchmaking in my last letter, although I must say that this Harry Gerard seems a bit old. Is he really so rich as to make his antiquity bearable? Do you like him? Or is this marriage solely Father's doing? A bright smile will compensate for a plain visage, I always said to you, but that is beside the point now, I suppose. A husband is a husband, and men are all very much alike, are they not? I barely see John, what with the Lords meeting in London, and the constant flurry of activity with the children. I so wish there was someone here to help me...

This letter joined its sister. A third, dated sometime later, began,

Dearest Lucy,

How sorry I was to hear that your promised husband succumbed to a fever and is no more. Horrid India! How relieved I will be to see you removed from that place. On a brighter note, I wish you very happy on your twenty-fifth birthday. As you recall, little Geoffrey's birthday is also this month. How time flies! Already he runs about and will soon be in breeches. Thank heavens, as baby Adelaide consumes much of my time. How good it will be to have you here. Poor Nurse Beckett is quite beside herself managing the older three, and as for Catherine and James, I fear they are running roughshod over our governess, a Miss Wortham, recently employed. Poor thing. She was brought up a gentlewoman, but alas, like so

140

many governesses, has come down in station and had to find employment. Is it not fortunate that you, dear sister, have family to take you in?

Yes indeed, Barton thought bitterly. How fortunate. His sleep that night was troubled. Barton dreamed he was a gull. The sea sang to him, each note a shimmer of purple and gray. He pushed toward the sun, closer and closer, its warmth like a woolen blanket upon his back. Then the breeze died, and he plummeted down to white-toothed waves. The wind caught him just in time. A fish jumped, and he snapped it up. He waltzed among the clouds until a ship sailed into view, and insatiable hunger drove him toward salt-rimed decks and bread crusts from weathered sailors.

His point of view changed, and suddenly he was a sailor. He smiled at a pair of gulls. They knew him and cawed fiercely. Though he could no longer understand their language, they spoke to some secret knowledge within him, whispering, freedom, freedom. The birds wheeled and drifted toward far-off cliffs painted a watercolor pink. Tossed like bits of paper, the gulls shrank until distance and forgetfulness consumed them.

***

Barton woke to the sound of loud voices overhead. Filaments of light pierced his tiny porthole, through which the minarets and mosques of Cádiz, Spain, were barely visible. The *Albion* bobbed at anchor.

He dressed and went above, where the first mate was just lowering a longboat into balmy waters. Two pastel parasols bloomed on a green sea and shrouded the boat's occupants, but he guessed Mrs. Leigh-Carlton and Miss Lucy must be among them. As it turned out, Mr. Charles Everly and Mr. Leigh-Carlton were also aboard, along with two sailors. The captain joined the man at the railing, saying, "If you want, we can pull 'er back up. Mr. Everly disembarks here, and the others de-cided to join him for a day ashore."

Glancing again toward the small boat, which now almost brushed the waves, Barton noticed a trunk occupying one end. Faint dismay took hold of him. He had not realized Mr. Everly would not be accompanying them all the way to England. "Nay," he told the captain, "It would be too tiring an outing for these old bones."

The captain slapped him on the back. "We are only as old as we feel, Mr. Barton."

Barton formed a smile but remained silent, watching as the boat was released and bucked along gentle waves, propelled by the two oar-wielding sailors. Other ships basked in the An-dalusian haze, and far off, a dock bustled with ant-sized work-ers. But Barton only had eyes for the shore-bound boat. Some-thing niggled at him—a sort of longing, or perhaps a memory. Feelings of loss tangled with a strange euphoria. He rubbed his temples, thinking he had better sit. The first mate brought him water and drew a deck chair into the shade of the foresail, asking if he felt unwell. He shook his head.

Barton lounged there even after the shadows withdrew and the harsh sun beat down on his head. He observed while another longboat drew up to shore and, later, returned with supplies and cargo bound for England. A deckhand mending sail nearby cast him occasional glances. Perhaps the man worried he might die of the heat, and the crew would be obliged to dispose of his remains.

Yet he felt oddly well. As morning stretched into afternoon, and the sun rose plump and joyful in a plate glass sky, those pulsing rays infused him with new energy. Life was not seep-ing out of him, as appearances might suggest; instead, it seeped into him. His mysterious and conflicted emotions battled, and gradually a boisterous feeling—the kind a youth experiences upon a virgin trip out into the world—overcame regret and sadness. He did not try to explain it, only soaked it in.

Not until sunset spilled across the horizon did the last boat return. Barton squinted, shaded his eyes, then absorbed what his subconsciousness had known long before. He thought of the seagulls from his dream. He thought of Miss Lucy and her letters, of Mr. Everly and his book about the female scientist and the summer birds. One pastel parasol appeared over the railing's edge. Mrs. Leigh-Cartlon's frizzy head emerged from under the lacy fringe. Barton waited. He envisioned a monarch butterfly landing briefly on the brim, mistaking it perhaps for a giant flower, then fluttering away into the dying light, a speck of color—smaller, smaller, gone.

Miss Lucy had flown.

There would be scandal, a fruitless search (he hoped), and finally, embarrassed forgetfulness. Miss Lucy's sister would sigh self-righteously when she chanced to remember her sibling, but Barton, from his small cottage in Shropshire, would smile as he gazed beneath the ruffled waves of the pond where he fished, and dreamed, and hoped.

Recessive Jeans
by Patricia Frolander

Stock dogs and horses are cowboys' best friends,
both have a trait wives do not.
Though the three can provoke a man to distraction,
the cow horse and dog won't get caught
in verbalization designed to confuse,
the logic that most men prefer,
like eating and working and cussing a bit,
that's natural, most males concur.

A man has his hands full doing his job,
fencing and cows take their toll.
There's springs to develop, corrals to be built,
check mares about ready to foal.
A dog earns respect when he follows commands,
saving hours of work for the boss,
in gathering bulls laid up in the brush
or findin' the calf that is lost.

A cowhorse that's savvy can save a man's life
when working with rough stock and such.
He reacts to the cowboy with no questions asked
responding to his gentle touch.
A woman's another concern altogether,
her logic can be quite perverse;
he's damned if he does and damned if he don't,
it's true menopause is a curse!

She likes the movies, dining and such;
he wants to stay by the fire.
She likes great novels, he likes "Cow Country;"
or sale bills on progeny sires.
A good hand of cards, team roping each week
sounds good to his way of thinking.
At a dance, she wants dancing, he wants to visit,
spin a yarn and do some beer drinking.

She cleans the house after dog hair and tracks
from cowboys who don't clean their boots,
bakes homemade pies, the laundry gets done,
she looks great in Levi's or suits.
She's good help with feeding or pulling a calf,
when gathering cows she's a hand,
life would be good, if he only could,
have her look like a woman and think like a man.

PART SIX

Thrum of Contentment

Waiting for Thimbleberries
by Kathy Bjornestad

It's been dry as a wind-scoured skeleton, the kind of dry where yellow grass crackles beneath your feet, where the only green in the yard comes from noxious thistle. Although it's only the start of July, forest fires ravage the West. Smoke masquerades as cloud cover and grays an otherwise blue morning sky. In the evening, a bloody sun sinks past parched hills.

So, this summer, I thought the thimbleberries wouldn't appear.

Last year, extra rainfall fooled the forest, made us all think we lived in damp northwestern climes where Mother Nature flaunts her greenery. In northeastern Wyoming, every plant is precious. The short growing season means you start corn in May and pray it doesn't freeze, coddle peppers indoors for a month, and buy watermelon at the store.

For the first time, we hiked into the hills and picked thimble-berries. I didn't know what they were at first. My husband looked them up on the Internet and discovered the following: thimbleberries are an edible, delicate, many-segmented fruit, red as rubies, with velvety leaves large as a man's palm, also called "woodsman's toilet paper." Indians used the leaves to treat ailments such as diarrhea, vomiting, dysentery, and ane-mia. The plant is rich in vitamin C.

What I discovered: You had to sweep the berry from its stem into your bucket gently, like a maid dusting fine china. You had to wade into the sea of bushes like a swimmer, arms raised, nudging green fronds aside while you navigated un-seen roots and brambles as carefully as a beach-goer wary of coral.

Cream-colored moths exploded before my incursive touch. Long-legged spiders scuttled away. During the search for the perfect bush, I quickly lost my husband and my Labrador. A splash of scarlet and I was off, veering further and further from the road and into white-barked aspen. Dappled shade splashed across undulating green. Somewhere above me, a squirrel scolded. My bucket filled. Red juices stained my fingers. A shaft of late-afternoon sunshine found me like a spotlight.

Suddenly, the bushes shook. I thought of bears, and my heart-beat quickened—but it was only the dog circling to check on me. I called out for my husband. Far away, like an echo, came his faint reply. Satisfied, I continued picking.

That was last year.

This year we suffer. My chickens pant in their coop. They'd sweat if they could. My dog droops behind me on our walk. Dust rises from our road and doesn't settle, but hangs in the air like white chalk beaten from an eraser.

The memory of rain is bittersweet. A single thundercloud brings on a sort of desperate nostalgia. Yet somehow our cherry bush sends new growth toward the sky. The buffalo grass grows. Baby wild turkeys waddle across our meadow, and new fawns rise from the prairie as though conjured.

And the thimbleberries flower.

Soon red fruit will punctuate their star-like borders. Online, you can buy thimbleberries for eight dollars a pound and one jar of jam for nine ninety-five, but I'll pick and can my own, taking a little piece of summer with me into winter.

Even a summer like this one.

It's been an odd year. Seventy degrees in March. Over one hundred in June. The ranchers despair for their hay crop. Fires turn thousands of acres into smoking ash. And I wonder if the rules are changing, our climate slipping more and more into unpredictable severity. But then I see flowering thimbleberry bushes. I'm reminded that I can't control Mother Nature. Like an avenging goddess, she'll wreak havoc where she will, but she'll also gift us with surprising beauty.

So, I watch patiently for the next cloud that might signal rain. Tend my garden. Move the chickens into deeper shade.

And wait for thimbleberries.

The Mycorrhizae
by Maria Lisa Eastman

It's still dark—cold.
The sun is coming around the curve,
spring thaw scents the wind.
Thick silence honeys my ears,
frozen air warms
as I climb to the top of the hill.

Below me, a chill river
weaves through familiar fields,
who can be troublesome, yes,
but always brilliant—
year after year, they call up a yield
like magic out of a tall black hat.

Now, they lie asleep,
their icy cover pulled close,
they dream in colors of
rain-dance, sunlight, hope.
Legions of small creatures
nest in sleeping soil—

the Mycorrhizac, fungal jewels
of garnet, sapphire, aquamarine.
They stir, whisper, conspire
with slumbering roots, unseen,
unnamed, and under the eager sun
they will soon ignite the grass skyward green.

These are the secret scholars of dirt,
who create living links, long equations,
whose solutions grow, tall,
into the rising air of summer's heat.

The Trees in Spring
by Constance Brewer

Even the trees talk to each other.
I hear Morse code in the leaves. Birds fill the gaps between
silences. Buds speak as quickly as they grow,

I'm just too slow to hear them. Years ago, we planted cottonwoods in the yard. One by one they withered until
only two remain, side by side.

The left shelters a nest and spreads its branches wide.
The right suffered winterkill and gamely drives suckers
amid deadwood. Each spring

I wait to see if new growth pops from dry twigs.
Each fall I hesitate, pruners in hand,
reluctant to sacrifice one precious limb.

Today I am content to listen as the trees speak
back and forth, and I hear the raspy throat of leaves punctuated by the trill of an early blackbird.

Saturday morning and you're up early.
You rake debris and old leaves from around the yard
before placing redwood mulch around the tree bases.

A soft clang rings as you hang a new copper feeder
from the right tree's stubborn branch. Birds pause, chirp, and
relay the message whispered by trees—

di dah di dit, dah dah dah, di di di dah, di.

L-o-v-e.

Resilient Friends
by Kathleen Smith

During my first winter of married life on the Davis Ranch in northern Campbell County, I developed a love affair with geraniums. Little did I know, when I met my first geranium, how important my flowers would become to my survival away from civilization. In our long-standing friendship, the plant taught me things about myself, and I discovered the flower's strengths. We are a match made in heaven—we both are ambitious workers, cold-weather resilient, and survivors with perennial optimism. While making my home on several ranches in Wyoming, I have discovered that geraniums and I will grow at all elevations, but both of us dislike the wind.

After moving to the country, I had a husband, horses, cows, and flowers. I planted annual and perennial beds with utter ignorance. My desire for color and blossoms meant selecting plants sold as bloomers for summer. I built my flower bed with time on my hands, caring for them as a mother would nurture a child. The geraniums were the focus of turning newly built terraces into displays of color. I planted, weeded, and watered. The earth called me to put my bare hands in the soil. I learned that growing plants involved building an intimate relationship with a particular place.

My first ranch yard beside the lava rock house built by the Wynkoop family of long ago consisted of a homesteader's yellow rosebush and an old purple lilac. Raspberry canes and two apple trees had been planted in the garden by the Davis Family. My flower beds were filled with petunias, marigolds, and geraniums of all colors and stages of bloom.

Visitors to our new home complimented my green thumb and blooming flower beds. Maybe because I lived fifty miles out in the country, bright colors became the only conversation topic among neighbors living along the miles of gravel roads, rocks, and grasses. Massive scarlet and magenta geraniums, purple petunias, and sunlight marigolds filled my rust-colored lava-scoria rock terraces along the house.

Many of my geraniums are four years old, with stems measuring half an inch in diameter. We have learned lessons and survived struggles growing together. The reassurance of seeing spring flowers after a long, cold winter provides beauty to a ranching landscape. Flowers, like people, are connected to their environment. Geraniums never die in southern Spain because the climate on the Mediterranean Ocean allows them to flower year-round. Foliage can grow six inches to three feet high and two feet wide. These flowers offer variation in color, but most come in white, pink, salmon, red, fuchsia, and lavender. And there are even a few bicolor. Geraniums have produced flowers every place both of us have lived and worked.

I take pride in where I have lived by mowing grass, straightening the out-of-place items, and at the end of the season, cleaning my flower beds. My one and only neighbor, Joni, gave me instructions on saving flowers for another year. After digging up my summer plants, I placed them in an upstairs, wide-sill bedroom window, with no curtains to shelter the direct southern January rays of sunshine. The room temperatures were cool. I read the leaves, touched the top of the soil in the pots, and hoped I was providing the correct care. As the calendar pages blew by like the weather, I remained inquisitive to determine if Joni's wintering advice was reliable. *Could the geraniums be saved for another year?* My neighbor was right. With proper winter care, geraniums will bloom again and are resilient companions. It is good to place my hands in the earth as I dig up geraniums to keep them over for winter, recycle, reuse, and reinvent their colorful blooms for another season.

Over the years, I have learned geraniums are ambitious; they do their job every day, as I do mine. I am a scholar when it comes to working. When I start ranch cleanup in the spring by lifting the heavy tire left by the gas tank or pieces of pipe from the men's building project, my muscles become sore. I'm soft, and some days resent working outside because I have been sheltered during the harsh winter. In early spring, when I remove my coat because the sun rays are too intense, wind-blown, and my lips chapped, I am not tanned. My tender skin burns. The geraniums' leaf edges are tender, too. They wind-burn in the hardening process after living a protected life in the south window. When the summer sun shines, the leaves grow healthy and strong, and the pink Martha Washington blooms are prolific. Martha is a loyal bloomer when water and fertilizer come at regular intervals. If my food and sleep are consistent, my energy levels explode in the spring. I work long days and get more jobs checked from my task list.

When the weather has more unsettled days with winds blowing, temperatures are cooler, and the Weather Channel proclaims the first frost warning is near. For me, it is time to make the last push to complete everything on my summer list. This means putting my geraniums to bed. After removing them from their summer location, I tuck my potted "geris" under the patio overhang for several days.

Then, I bring my favorite work companions inside to the window. They receive fertilizer and water a couple of times during October. I get busy with holiday plans and forget to pluck the faded, withered blooms and curled-up leaves that result from shorter days. On one of the last days of October, they are watered, and they gift their last set of blooms. By November, they are beginning to hibernate; they receive less water, then around the New Year, and again on Valentine's Day. Every part of the soil is drenched to ensure my geris' roots are soaked. Some years they get enough sun for their leaves to be green, lush, fuzzed, and soft. If cloudy winter days bring a bit less light, every third leaf will be prominent and growing. Either way, the watering works. I have learned by accident when I've not stored them away in the fall, these resilient flowers can survive frost and temperatures as low as twenty-five degrees.

I left my mark on the Davis Ranch with the flower terraces my neighbor, Joni, and I built. I am sure the following spring, after I moved on to the Moorcroft ranch, the biannual marigolds reseeded with only nature's care. I didn't do the best I could have with friendships, but I sent Christmas cards most years, and my flowers bloomed every summer on a different ranch, in a new location with memories of neighbors and the ranch I left behind.

Friendships with living things like animals and humans bloom in much the same way; geraniums blossom with kindness, gentle tending, and common soil. With neighbors, we have the additional connection of listening. We even listen to our animals, but we watch our plants which is a form of listening and being aware of where they are in their life cycle. Flowers and friendships are sentient beings; they are responsive to sensory impressions. Their connections to me and the companionship they've offered have journeyed with me throughout my life.

Blessed
by John R. Gutiérrez

We spent some time talking, laughing, and reminiscing,
me wishing I could have done more.
She told me she had worked since the age of ten,
living alone while mama knew nothing—didn't care.
"Blessed, I was," she said.

At fifteen she moved to the country,
lived alone in a one-room house,
ran a wire from a pole to home,
for heat, to cook, to look and see.
"Blessed, I was," she said.

At twenty-two, alone again,
she made money, did what she wanted—
but trying times buried her:
school, marriage, divorce.
"Blessed, I was," she said.

She paid for the meal we shared.
We hugged, friendship renewed.
I felt her heart beating in mine.
I let go to hear her whisper.
"Blessed I am," she said.

Alive
by James Bowers

Now is the vicious time of the year when the temperature rises above 100 degrees; the green grass dries into crisp, brown blades; and the clouds, lit by electric flashes of light, remain impotent. The creek has stopped running, its bed clogged with fallen trees, the wreckage of early spring snowstorms. The county road swirls with dust behind each passing car, but in the ditch are delicate bluebells as well as purple thistles, memorials to the endurance of beauty in an arid world.

As my wife and I walk along the road seldom harassed by vehicles, we find ourselves transported to another time, another place, a memory embedded in a world of imagination, where sequoia in California thrust heavenward their cathedral branches as we walked on the soft, moist carpet of needles and wondered at the light shining through the mist far above our heads. We were young then, our oldest child an infant strapped to my back, our future still beckoning and unknown.

Although we lived in the city, we were not then, nor have ever been, civilized. We are creatures born of Mother Earth and find our home in her embrace. How often during the intervening years have we followed one another along a narrow, winding path in the woods, stepping over fallen logs, sidestepping pools of water, then tripping over obtruding rocks because we were too busy noticing the leaves on the trees, the flowers protruding through the moss? Silence and mystery have followed us all our days as each new turn on the path has revealed the excitement of the unexpected, the beauty of the unknown.

Yes, now we find ourselves on an arid road, elderly citizens whose earthly bodies must soon be scattered as ashes to the winds. Our future has become a past full of unforgettable moments. But in our imaginations, we have never aged. We are forever that young couple with their newborn child, arrested by beauty wherever it is found. The mystery of the unknown still beckons. We are curious about the new life that awaits us after death. We peer through the dust and see the light shining far above. In the meantime, each new day is a gift, an opportunity once again to absorb the beauty of the trees, the flowers; to relive the memories as stories retold to our children, our grandchildren, our friends. Our bodies may be exhausted by the heat; nevertheless, we are eternally alive.

Unexpected Grace
by Constance Brewer

The flash of tail lights ahead, our line of vehicles slows.
Soon we grind to a halt, mobile mess to parking lot.
Lights flash as an ambulance creeps down the shoulder.
I crane my head, see nothing, so far back in the pack my
view is a wall of cars and trucks. Time ticks, music plays
rock, and I sit and wait. After 20 minutes I shut the car off.
Another 10 and I roll down the window, early morning sun
heating glass and leather. One by one vehicles around me
ping from idle to stop. We're here for the long haul.
Off the shoulder, a barbed-wire fence, beyond that a thicket
of trees and man-made pond. Cows graze a gentle slope.
Overhead, a hawk soars and rides the currents. Folding
wings, it stoops and dives into the pasture. Minutes pass as I
watch, rapt. The bird struggles aloft, carrying its dangling
prey, flapping for home, and hungry mouths to stuff full. Air
wafts—exhaust and dirt, the tang of faded rain. Black cows
amble in a long line to the pond to drink and I catch a two-
tone low from a straggler as a meadowlark bursts into song.
It's pleasant to sit, ignore being late to work,
ignore anything but the scene in my passenger
window, framed in blue, how it plays out whether
I'm stopped or driving, never asking for my attention,
not noticing the calm thrum of my contentment.

Autumn (a translation)
by Viktoriia Peterson

Light rain is autumn crying.
Droplets tap on the bright foliage.
Misty gray covers the river.
My father leaves a chain of footprints on the wet sand.
Fish splash beneath the river's cold surface.
A yellow leaf sticks to the grass.
Flocks of ducks in annual flight
Gather there in the blue.

My father walks along the cherished path
Along the water, light spinning rod on hand.
An autumn day, an hour before dawn,
He comes to the river.
He loves this wet autumn—
Light rain, the smell of rotten leaves

Well, what are we left with?
We will remain with what we love,
The thoughts we have.
That sometimes saves us from darkness.
Fine rain, colorful autumn
The splash of water, the smell of wet foliage.

PART SEVEN

Together is a Compliment

"Are You Kidding Me?" and "Instructions for Dad's Breakfast" (excerpts.) *Breakfast with Dad during a Pandemic: A Cynical Daughter's Guide to Living with a Grumpy, Sad Old Man Who Misses His Wife and Wants to Die* (work in progess)
by Morgan Callan Rogers

Are You Kidding Me?

It is 4:28 a.m. on Thursday morning, January 28, 2021. I am up preparing my 92-year-old dad's breakfast while he showers. I am not fond of this hour. In fact, I don't recognize it at all. I like to sleep in till 8:00 a.m. or so. Dad is one of those freaks who gets up really early because…? "Reminds me of the Army," he said.

Winter has marched in with a big old blizzard. Something else has marched in as well—a medical pandemic called Covid 19. We have been 'locked down' and 'masked' since March 20, 2020. I moved in with him right before the world was declared closed due to illness. Neither of us expected this to happen, but he isn't well, and I am his unmarried 68-year-old daughter, and he asked me to move in because he didn't want to go to a 'home'. He wants to die 'at home'. The day after I moved in, the Covid 'lock-down' took place. I went into my parents' room, gazed at a picture of my mother on the wall, and said, "ARE YOU KIDDING ME?" She just smiled back. My father also speaks to her photo when he goes to bed. "Night, Fran," he says. I can hear him say it from my nearby bedroom. It breaks my heart.

Every other day is shower day for my dad. On those days, he clambers over the rim of the tub, lowers himself onto a plastic chair, and gives himself a shower. I stay near the closed bathroom door, listening to make sure he doesn't fall. He's a modest man and he's a stubborn man. It embarrasses him when I have to help. But I am all he has if he falls or has an accident. Once, a few years back, before my mother died, my sister and

164

I suggested they put in a walk-in shower with a seat. "What for?" my dad growled. By then, my 90-year-old mother was too tired to argue, so she, too, scrambled over the edge of the tub for the safety of the bath chair, until the day before she died of a heart attack that she refused to acknowledge before it was too late.

It's dark outside and cold, and my cat is crying because she's hungry. Always, about food. I just fed her, but it's not enough. So, we begin a battle of wills. She will win, of course, and I will dump kibble into the dish to shut her up. When Dad is done with his shower, I lead the cat to our bedroom, and I will shut the door. Dad doesn't like cats; never has. Once, he drowned a bunch of kittens and their mother. He stuffed them into a burlap bag, rowed out to the middle of a river, and dropped the bag filled with squirming cats into the water. Later, he made it known that he had enjoyed it. When I moved in, I told him I would not move in without my cat. He tolerates her and she's not friendly to begin with, so they avoid each other whenever they can.

I never meant for this to happen. My plan was to be married, living somewhere comfortably far away, where I could come home on occasions and bring part of my own family, complete with noisy, irresistible kids. Plans change, and change is the only thing that's certain, so, no kids, no home away, no spouse, no excuse not to be helpful. Mom died, and here I am. My sister is the one who has the family, and she lives only seven miles away. My brother lives halfway across the country, with his wife. It's me. And him. And Covid. Dad's response to it all is, "Well, whoopie!" He says this sarcastically, apropos of something that has irked him.

Well, whoopie. Yeah.

Instructions For Dad's Breakfast

When Dad has survived his shower, he pushes his walker toward the kitchen. I have, by this time, put the cat into my bedroom and shut the door and turned on AM radio to the nostalgia station, which takes me back into my early and teenage years. Every song reminds me of something that has happened in my life, both good and bad.

It took me weeks to get his breakfast ritual straight. It's not hard, on paper.

Take his dark blue cereal bowl. Fill it with cereal, "Oat Honeys," or something like that. Put it on the table. Pour his pills into a little red plastic cup and put it on the table in back of the blue bowl. Put out a napkin. Place a spoon for the cereal on the napkin, between the bowl and his coffee mug. Heat up water for instant, decaf coffee. Pour the hot water into a mug that reads, "Work is for people who don't know how to play golf." Slip a spoonful of sugar and a bloop of hazelnut creamer into the cup. Place the mug on the table. Put the plain or molasses donut on the table between the mug and cereal bowl.

Have I mentioned that my father is almost completely blind from glaucoma and macular degeneration? So, there is a need to set things in their proper places. Also, he was in the Army and loved it, and there's that to consider. Order. Must. Have. Order. Only, I am absent-minded, usually roaming some inner landscape or wishing I was still in bed, or wondering how I ended up where I am and why this path has led me to elder care in my hometown. At any rate, I always forget something, usually the cereal teaspoon or the milk for the cereal. Sometimes, Dad is amused by my forgetfulness. Or sometimes, he'll say, "Fa chrissake! You goofy or something?" And I'll jump up and scurry to make amends.

We make cursory talk during breakfast. I dread this, as I run out of talk after 'Good morning.' I hate myself because I feel

166

so uncomfortable and so filled with a strange disappointment in myself. I wish I didn't, but I do. There are reasons for that, and they may come up, and they may not. I have just started this memoir, and I am not certain what will remain standing after I have sifted through it a hundred times. So, I sit opposite him, in Mom's old chair, and I'm not Mom, and I blame myself for that, too. I try calming exercises, deep breathing, little bits of talk. But then, some song like "It's My Party and I'll Cry If I Want To" plays on the radio and I think about my cousin Jane, and how she likes that song and how she has cancer, and I want to step out onto the porch for a minute and shout to the cold earth and far-away sky, "Fa chrissake! You goofy or something?"

Waiting for Noche
by Maria Lisa Eastman

I'm not thinking about her.
I'm surprised at myself.

Instead, I worry about the hovering storm,
the temperatures, roads slicked in ice,
the muddy corrals where she stands,
and about the man who will sell her to me
this morning at seven sharp before he drives to church.
I'll run my hand down her legs,
and, if she'll let me, I'll put my fingers
into her dove mouth to check her teeth.
He will reach into his coat, hand me her papers.
I'll read again that she was a winner,
that she won a ton of money,
that they sent her to Keeneland,
where only the finest are sold.

Somehow, she landed on a ranch out here,
produced foals every year, and they won too,
kept the cash flowing into the pockets of plain people
who loved to watch them run.
An aged mare now, she can't carry another foal,
anyone could tell the ad in the classifieds
was a barely-veiled swan song.
I saw it some time ago, let it go—
too busy, too many, too much.

But here I am this morning
waiting for the sun to come up
outside my hotel room
while down the road a few miles
she already knows something's different.
I'll thank the man for selling her to me,
pay the brand inspector.

I'll slip the black halter on her head,
turn to lead her into the trailer.
I'll let their disbelief bounce off my back,
tell her not to worry.
We'll drive over the high pass through the snow,
head home where all the others
already know something has changed.

Now it's their turn,
they are the ones waiting for Noche.

Love Poem with Accolades
by Constance Brewer

It's hell growing old. You age out of flattery.
No one tells you you're pretty anymore.
The athletes you watch play ball could be
your grandchildren.

Somehow, young waitresses now call you *honey*,
and *dear*, and *sweetie*, and point you to the senior special.
In my head I'm twenty-five, no more than thirty-two.
My body has a different perception
as it strives to do all I ask.

And then there is us. We've been together far too long. You
don't say 'hey beautiful' anymore, but nor do you notice the
increasing silver strands in my dark hair.

Yesterday you bought me a new lamp with LED bulbs
bright enough to knit black yarn by.
Maybe you saw me struggle to count my stitches. Maybe you
hate the heavy cheater glasses I need to wear.

Either way, it's beautiful, what you did, and I
have to remember to tell you so.

Each day together is a compliment.

Ranch Rituals
by Jean Helmer

I am ranch, one of a unique breed of folks who, by birth, are baptized into the covenantal relationship that exists between people, land, crops, livestock, and the Creator. The covenant "take care of God's land and critters, and trust God to take care of you" had been bred into the marrow of my bones generations before the phrases "carbon footprint" and "organic farming" were uttered. I was taught to identify plants and animals and to know their patterns of growth and behavior. I also inherited the rites and rituals of stewardship and neighborliness.

The May Ritual

Mom's birthday and Mother's Day often coincided. While my parents rarely acknowledged special days with physical gifts, they freely gave the gifts of time and thoughtfulness. The May ritual always began with a twinkle in Dad's blue eyes and a grin tugging at his lips.

"Thought I'd run up to the back pasture to see how the grass is coming. Go look to see how long before we can turn the cattle back there. Ya wanna ride along?"

Dad's words spurred us into action. Mom's face lit up.

"Let me get a bucket," she replied, "the bluebells ought to be out."

Thus, it began. We climbed into the pickup, Dad at the wheel, Mom in the passenger seat, Danny and I standing in the pickup box near the cab where we could hang on through the open window of the door. If it had rained the day before, we would take a swing across the hillside in the first pasture to check for mushrooms. We kept a sharp lookout from our vantage point in the back, looking for badger holes that might break the leg of an unwary cow. At the east gate, Dad stopped. Mom opened the gate and then stretched it shut after Dad had driven through. Then our ascent began into the pine-dotted foothills of the northern Black Hills. We paralleled the fence line checking for breaks and loose wires. At the back dam, Dad stopped and shut off the engine. "I'm going to slip up top and walk the fence." He indicated the direction of his travels with a sideways nod of his head. "You guys look around for cockleburs, locoweed, and larkspur," he'd direct us. Mom led our search.

The area around the dam where the cattle had trampled the ground the previous summer was prime territory for undesirable plants. Cocklebur is poisonous to livestock in its two-leaf stage. Locoweed's flowers are a pretty pink, larkspur's deep purple, but the plants are deadly to livestock. As soon as Mom found one of the plants, she'd call us over to have a close look to remind us exactly what we were seeking. We marked the cockleburs so Dad could dig them later. Locoweed has a brittle nature, so pulling it from the roots whenever we found it usually controlled the plant. Larkspur was sparse in our pasture so simply picking all of its pretty purple blossoms kept it under control.

"Do you smell that?" Mom asked.

"Smell what?" I asked.

"Stop. Concentrate. Use your nose. What do you smell?"

I sniffed the air. Something tickled my senses. Closing my eyes, I inhaled deeply while slowly turning my head. "What is it?"

"Plums. They're blooming. I can smell them. Let's go check the draw." Soon she had her jackknife out and we cut a few branches. "See this," she said, pulling a branch near for a closer observation. "You can see the buds forming. We'll cut some of these. When we put them into water, they will open up into full bloom."

Dad returned from fence checking and we went into the high country. The grass was lush on the high meadow floor. We kept our eyes peeled for the first sighting of blue or magenta. Mom always spotted the colors first. The first bluebells and shooting stars made spring official. Dad would stop, and we would pick flowers for bouquets.

"Remember," Mom admonished, "it's one for the bugs, one for seed, and one for me." Thus we learned our earliest lessons in conservation. Unless it was larkspur, we were never to pick a single flower. There always had to be at least three separate plants blooming. Then, we could pick one stem of flowers from every third plant.

While we were picking flowers, Dad continued his journey checking fence lines. When he returned from the back boundary fence lines, Mom sent Danny and me to get into the pickup, then handed me the bucket of flowers to hold. We returned to the lower pasture. This time when we stopped at the gate, Dad said, "Leave it open. The grass is far enough along and the back dam is full. The cattle might as well spread out."

Mom stretched the gate back against the barbed wire and tucked the post into the top wire so livestock would not get tangled in it.

Our adventure ended at the dam by the artesian well. Danny and I checked for snails. Dad checked the water pipes. Mom checked the garden site. It was one acre fenced out of the pasture and lined with cherry trees. Separating the wooly roots of buffalo grass from the soil was tedious work, but once released, the high plains soil combined with artesian water made for a productive garden. Within a few days, we would return to plant the garden and to transplant the tomatoes Mom had started by the east windows on the porch.

Back at the house, we made bouquets of flowers. One bouquet for church at Aladdin, one for Hay Creek School on Monday, one for an elderly neighbor who could no longer climb hills, and the final one for Aunt Katherine whose pine-covered hillsides ran to crocus instead of shooting stars and bluebells.

The Late Spring Rains Ritual

Ranch kids do not go barefoot. Barefoot is for town kids with lush lawns and smooth sidewalks. We had sparse gravel, a scraggly crop of June grass interspersed with chickweed, sharp rocks, and occasionally the even sharper puncture vine. Beyond the yard was the board pile of old lumber where rusty nails lurked. Rattlesnakes often traveled through the area, and there was always the risk of livestock stepping on an unwary kid's foot. Nope. Ranch kids do not go barefoot.

But, when it rained hard enough to leave puddles in the yard and lane, that all changed. By late afternoon on the third day, or early morning on the fourth day, we were told to go barefoot. It was our job to walk into each puddle and stomp the green foam of growing mosquito eggs into the soft clay at the bottom of the puddles. This method of mosquito eradication killed the larvae without using any chemicals. As we stomped, summer happiness oozed beneath our feet and squished up between our toes.

The Thunderstorm Ritual

Even now, decades after moving to town, my return to the ageless ranch rituals learned in childhood is prompted by long, hot summer nights. At some subtle, nameless change in the wind outside the sealed windows of my air-conditioned house, I rise, moving softly so as not to disturb my husband. He was raised on a farm. Those growing up on irrigated flat land do not learn the ritual.

I go first to the south window, peer through the blinds, and then I walk—stalking, pacing from window to window, checking, checking, squinting eyes to see beyond the yard, beyond the neighbor's houses. I move in the old pattern, from window to window, clockwise. Pace. Pause. Peer. Pace. Pause. Peer.

"Good grief, Beula Jean," my husband's sleep-thick voice mutters.

But my energies are focused in another direction, on other sounds. Nineteen miles distant, I am certain I hear my sister's footfalls as she climbs the stairs to her second-story windows, where she begins at the south glass patio doors and moves clockwise through the rooms. Her eyes squint to see beyond the yard, to see through the trees. She scans the hills, searches the clouds, and smells the air at each window just as I do. We inherited the ritual from the land, learned the walk from our mother when we were children, when we lived up Hay Creek.

"What are you doing?" I had asked my mother as I heard her moving through the darkened house during my early youth.

"Just checking the windows. Go back to sleep."

But I couldn't. Something was there in the wind, something that wouldn't let me fall back asleep. I got up and joined her, positioning myself at the second window in the living room. Heat lightning sheeted across the south hills, silhouetted thunderheads.

"When you see a flash of lightning, keep your eyes on that spot. Watch to see if there is a red glow," Mom directed me. Then she moved to the west window. The walk had begun.

A subtle, nebulous change in the lightning called Dad to join the ritual. Rising, he began at the south windows, stared intently at the hills in the back pasture, willed the darkness to hold together. He'd glance only briefly to the west and the north. By now lightning flashes split the dark. Lightning that began high in the sky was met halfway by bolts that seemed to leap from the earth.

"Imagine it's time. Better get started." He pulled on his blue chambray shirt and the denim bib overalls he'd worn that day, crunched across the gravel by the back door, and backed the pickup to the shed. Metal clanking against metal punctuated the thunder as he loaded cream cans, shotgun cans, barrels, anything which would hold water. He flipped the garden hose into the first can as he loaded gunny sacks and seed sacks. While the second can filled, he loaded shovels, rakes, and an axe. He worked automatically; his restless eyes swept the sur-rounding hills. By now, the hose alone was too slow. His hands dipped a milk pail into the stock tank; water splashing each container to fullness. His eyes traced lightning bolts to the ground, analyzed each strike carefully.

Inside, Mom and I paced in sequence and watched, paced and watched, freezing at each flash of lightning, riveting our eyes to the spot where the flash originated, praying that no yellow ball or red glow would follow. We paced and sniffed. Our noses sorted and identified the odors. Bruised pine meant hail in the Bear Lodge. Bruised sage, hail on Sourdough Flats to the northwest. Bruised alfalfa told of hail up Sandy Draw. Sul-fur meant a lightning bolt on the ground. We paced clockwise from window to window. We paused, peered into the deep darkness, sniffed, and rotated to the next window, restlessly, relentlessly.

Outside, Dad paused by his loaded pickup, his fingers pulling the Prince Albert tobacco can and a cigarette paper from the front pocket of his bib overalls. A farmer-match flared briefly in the darkness as he lit his hand-rolled cigarette. His lean form was silhouetted by intermittent lightning flashes. "Going up top," he called. His pickup rolled past the barns. Minutes or perhaps only seconds later, he returned. Engine running, tires still moving, he opened his door and shouted, "Ruth, get on the horn. Got one going up over the rimrock. Looks like it's on Kirksey's 80." His door slammed and he was gone.

Mom hurried to the telephone, took the earpiece out of its cradle, and began cranking a general ring. This single, long ring on the party-line summoned all who heard it. In the darkened room, the voices of neighbors came over the phone. They identified themselves as they answered. "Hutchinsons." "Heetlands." "Sipes." "McKays."

When the voices paused, Mom leaned close to the mouthpiece. "This is Fishels. Floyd spotted a fire up on the flats. He thinks it's Kirksey's south 80." Still tethered to the phone on the wall, she turned, resuming her watch as she listened. Shortly she said, "I'll ring off then." She returned the earpiece to its hook. "Grace says they can see flames from there. The fire's between them and Sissons."

We returned to the windows safe in the knowledge that menfolk were converging on the fire with water, sacks, shovels, anything that could be used to beat down or smother flames, or to clear a fire line that flames could not cross. Other men, selected by a nameless, unspoken code, stayed behind, watching, waiting for the next general ring, the next fire. And in the houses throughout the neighborhood, the womenfolk resumed their walk.

The Chickens' Christmas Ritual

My folks had 900 acres along Hay Creek on the South Dakota/Wyoming border. Most ranch kids have animals to call their own. You know, a horse, a dog, cats—the standard critters. We had a horse—an old workhorse. Sitting on her back was like straddling a barn. But I couldn't ride her in the winter. In the winter she was pastured in the creek bottom hay fields with the cattle. There was a ranch dog, but Herman was little brother Danny's steady companion, not mine. Cats? Sure, but they were barn cats—working cats. They had a job to do—mouse prevention. Fiddle with 'em too much, they'd get lazy, wouldn't hunt. Or grow too attached, they'd get distemper and die. That left chickens. The chicken coop, an old claim shack positioned at the top of the bank of Hay Creek, was my winter domain.

Twice daily I got "togged up" in my winter coat, overshoes, scarf, and mittens and went to do my chores. Taking two metal buckets, one of milk and another of warm water, I'd head for the chicken coop. These buckets had a habit of bumping my legs and filling my overboots until I learned to hold the buckets away from me as I walked. It made them heavier and harder to carry, but that was better than wet socks and frozen overshoes. Twenty yards later, I set the buckets by the chicken coop and went to the granary for a third bucket of ground barley. Back at the coop, buckets in proper order, I'd take a deep breath and open the door.

Opening the door always caused a storm of panic. Wings churned billows of dust, and beaks squawked end-time tidings as old biddies fled for the back of the coop. Once there, the Rock Island Red tidal wave would reverse and sweep forward, coming to a swirling stop around the buckets. One or two pets would hasten to my feet and crouch, waiting to be picked up.

"R-r-right, r-r-right" they seemed to cluck as I patted their bronze backs. Greetings completed, I emptied litter from the galvanized troughs that sat on the floor and filled them with ground barley. Then, the *pièce de résistance*, I poured still warm-from-the-cows milk over the barley and mixed it into a mash. Wing-flapping into position, the chickens feasted as I filled waterers and gathered the eggs.

During sub-zero cold snaps, I would break bales of straw and scatter them on the floor to provide some warmth in the uninsulated building. Sometimes I was directed to scatter wheat in the midst of the straw. "That will give the chickens something to scratch for," said my folks, "keep them from getting bored." Whether it was boredom or something else, searching for wheat decreased the cannibalism that sometimes causes chickens to select a timid member of the flock and peck at it until it bleeds. Left long enough, this "bottom of the pecking order" chicken will be killed by its coop mates—a tough thing for a kid to see happen in the "kindly" world of animals, but a valuable lesson for life, nevertheless.

Whether it was to alleviate the chickens' boredom or my own, I'm not certain, but one December, I began feeling sorry for those chickens. It had been a particularly long winter. The chickens seemed sad. It was as though they had given up hope of ever seeing spring.

"Listlessness," I would call it once I was old enough to be familiar with the term.

Country school dismissing for vacation signaled the start of our holiday ritual. We would take a run up into the back pasture to cut a jack pine for our Christmas tree. This tree would sit in a bucket of water in our enclosed back porch awaiting Christmas Eve when it would get decorated just in time for Santa's annual trip. It was on this trek into the back pasture that my idea was born.

"Dad, can I have a tree?" I asked.

"Don't need more than one; they're fire hazards."

"I wouldn't put it in the house. I'd put it in the chicken coop."

Dad gave me a measured look and shook his head, but when we got back to the house, I discovered that there was an extra-large branch left in the pickup after he took our tree into the back porch.

That night after chores, my brother and I sat at the living room table making decorations—red and green paper chains and strings of popcorn. Finally, we had enough to cover our tree. But I wasn't finished.

"Can we make more popcorn?"

"What for?" asked Mom.

"'Cuz I'm making a tree for the chickens," I explained.

"Tomfoolery," chuckled Mom, and she began popping more corn.

The next morning after the animals had been fed, the cows milked, and our own breakfast was done, I was ready to fix Christmas for the chickens.

"Since you're going to be out there playing, you might as well take these potato peelings and orange peels along with you. The chickens need the vitamins. Their eggs are getting pale," said Mom as she sent me out the door with the scrap bucket.

I stashed the scraps by the coop, dragged the branch out of the pick-up and went to the board pile. A search yielded enough lumber for a crude stand, then it was off to the chickens.

As I opened the door, the standard tidal wave broke. The chickens froze in position, torn between the need to flee and the desire to continue eating the mash delivered earlier.

"Brought you a tree," I announced to their sudden silence and set the tree by the window. My homemade stand shuddered, disintegrated, and the wall caught the Christmas offering and held it at a rakish angle.

"Wha-a-a-at?" asked one old biddy, leading the others. "Wha-a-a-at? Wha-a-a-at?"

A few brave souls ventured forward for a closer look as I hung the popcorn rope, added orange rind ornaments and a potato peel tree skirt, and stepped back to admire my effort. "Well, it does improve the place," I announced.

"Wha-a-a-at?" an old hen repeated.

"Wha-a-a-at yourself," I beamed, impressed with my magnanimity. "Even chickens deserve to have Christmas."

A rooster crowed his agreement.

The Family Rate
by Constance Brewer

My son leans into his work, intent on the truck engine, a
problem to be puzzled out, a tangled mystery to solve. Lost
in mechanical mindfulness, the world outside fades to white
noise broken by the ratchet of a wrench. A black canvas
work bag holds the tools needed for this month's fix. He
hums under his breath as he works, grease sliding over his
knuckles, transferred to cheek as he absentmindedly rubs his
face. Solutions flip through his mind like a game of solitaire.
The loose bolt card, the electrical card, the faulty distributor
card. He reaches into the work bag and grabs the right tool.
Disconnecting wires, he sets parts on the hood ledge, pokes
around, raises a hand in triumph. A gentle *Ah-ha* and he
turns to me with a grin, meditative inquiry complete. A
faulty spark plug. He's happy to fix it, solve the problem,
help his mother. Another job accomplished with skills he's
honed over the years, trial and error; where hands-on learning beats book knowledge. He replaces the plug, closes the
hood, starts the truck. It hums. He's pleased, and it's time to
place the tools back in their assigned slots, wipe hands on a
greasy rag, flash a smile. He hugs me goodbye, mindful of
the dirty fingers, mission complete, satisfaction high as he
refuses the money I try to shove into his hand.

"The Sunday Mare" (revised excerpt). *Arizona Tough: Of Men and Horses*
by Dawn Newland

"Good morning, John. I thought it best to let you know, today's the last Sunday I'll be visiting you here. I've decided to go with Jimmer after all."

A groan escapes her as Lucy Tressler leans on the grave marker and lowers herself to sit. Her neighbor, Jim Thornhill, and his cowboys came early last spring to lay sod over the raw earth mound. It's green now. John's baby, like his daddy, is impatient, and kicks at his confines. Lucy's one hand cradles her large belly. The other traces the dash between the dates carved in the rough pine. She reads aloud. "Born 1870 – Died February 1, 1896. John Curry, killed by Jim Winter."

And she ponders the dash. "Oh, my Johnny, twenty-six years is not nearly enough time. It's still hard to believe that I'll never hear you blasting through the door, exasperated, crying out, 'Christ sakes, M' Lady, what were you thinking?' And then your howling laugh. Always your laugh, John. I've heard living alone in this vast land can drive a woman mad. I talk to you like this to keep my sanity."

Lucy's laugh is nervous today. "John, I fear Jim Winter and Ab Gill have won my land. You fought for me, but they are here to stay, and so are the sheep and the plows."

She stares off to the far western skyline, her mind lost in thought. At length she ponders, "Why on earth do these men have to come to me at night? I haven't had a good night's rest since this scorching heat started. First, it's you, John, and your booming laugh. Then it's Jim, saying 'Marry me. Do this, do that.' Even my old husband, Daniel, showed up in my dreams throwing punches. If that wasn't enough torment, he took this baby from me, like he did my first five. Maybe I dreamed of him because it's just now coming up on July 7th, a year since he near killed me and stole the children." Lucy cringes as she recalls the horror of the past year.

The handful of purple crazyweed she gathered on her walk seems appropriate, as does talking to a dead man. "You know, Rock Creek could have been Crazy Woman Creek last summer, had it not been for you. You saved me from myself, time and again. Talked me back from the edge of insanity. You, wild John Curry, of all people." Lucy laughs hollowly and lays the purple flowers at John's marker before struggling to her feet.

"I've worked hard at staying on the homestead, John. You've surely watched from your perch with the angels. Have you ever seen such a bitter spring here on the High Line of Montana? The snow run-off, out of the Little Rockies, near washed Landusky out of the valley." Lucy pauses before adding, "I believe Jim is coming for me today, and I'm going with him. I can't think of anyone better to help raise this child. If he is as wild as you and as crazy as I, he'll be a handful. And John, the thing is, I love Jim. Like I love you."

A horseman lopes up from the purple shadows of Siparyann Creek far to the west. Lucy picks up her skirts and hurries toward home. She recites her worries to the meadowlarks as she runs. "This being the Independence weekend, I worried that he'd not come. But Jim Thornhill is surely a man that can be counted on to do what he says."

As has been his custom, every Sunday since February 1, the day John was shot, Jim rides in on the buckskin mare. He is methodical in his actions as he dismounts, drops the bridle, and hobbles her to graze. He fusses with loosening his cinch and hanging his bridle just so. Jim wears his Sunday best, like he's going to church. In his long, easy stride, he saunters across the yard toward Lucy. His face is worry-worn, stern, a touch hard. His eyes are soft and speak more than his words do.

"Ahem … morning Missus Tressler," he calls out as he comes, "and a fine one it is." Jim's voice is pleasant and strong. Stopping in front of her, feet apart in typical stockman fashion, he hooks a thumb in the top of his well-oiled leather cartridge belt. After removing his hat, Jim smooths his dark hair, clasps the Stetson in his hands in front of him, and he waits—like he does every Sunday.

"Morning, James. Sunday? So soon? It sneaked right up on me." It's a lie, of course, but Lucy holds her composure.

"You are particularly easy on my eyes this mornin'," Jim drawls. "The dress suits you, matches your purt-near greens."

Him referring to her eyes seals her suspicion that he's the one that left the dress and supplies on her doorstep. "My 'purt-near greens' used to be one of your weaknesses, and you haven't many." Lucy laughs softly, "And you have cleaned up rather well yourself, James." Lucy stifles her smile. Jim is handsome beyond reason. He can have any woman he wants. Why on earth he still insists on having her is a mystery, although a comfort.

"Are you ready?" he asks.

"For what, James?"

"To marry me, Lucy. Same question as always."

"What if I said 'yes' this morning? What then?" Jim's eyes sparkle with surprise and no small amount of pleasure. His mustache twitches at the corners, hinting at a smile. "My, my," Lucy exclaims, "I haven't seen that frown leave your face in a coon's age."

Jim clears his throat. "Reckon I could use a cup of coffee. Maybe make us a plan."

"Mind you, James, I didn't say yes. I asked 'what if?' I have not yet been able to get a divorce from Daniel, though Lord knows I've tried."

"We'll take care of Daniel Tressler in due time."

"One thing I'll say for you, James, you are persistent."

"Is that a compliment?" he asks, letting the smile fully escape from under the well-trimmed mustache.

"Take it how you will."

"I'll take it any way I can get it." Jim reaches across the months of misunderstandings to draw Lucy to his chest. He seems to not mind that her belly hits him in the belt buckle. He near groans her name. "Aw, Lucy, it's been too darned long."

"It has, Jim. There's so much between us and so much that separates us." She breathes into his neck, quivering in the strength of his embrace. "I hope we are not being fools in thinking we can ever be the same again."

"Not the same. We'll be the better for having been down this road."

"You always know what to say. How can you be so sure?"

"Life isn't for sure on much, except being alone is hell. As long as I have a breath left in me, I'll be here, for you."

Nerves trigger what John calls Lucy's idle prattle. "It's been too warm to have a fire. I haven't felt much like eating of late. I apologize, I didn't even make coffee. The smell is unsettling to my stomach. I did, however, put together a picnic lunch. I'll fetch it if that is agreeable to you."

Pulling away from Jim, Lucy hurries into the cabin. After picking up the lunch basket, she leans a moment at the table, working at gathering her wits. Her thoughts erupt in the self-chatter she has become so used to. "Oh, he still has the same unearthly power he's always had. What a relief! Time, tragedy, and me carrying John's child has not changed anything between us. If anything, our love feels stronger." Lucy turns to see Jim leaning on the door frame. He is grinning, and everything about him fills the space completely.

"Shall we mosey to the creek for the picnic?" Jim asks in his slow drawl.

A wave of relief washes over her at hearing that voice, rich, slow as honey. Like his walk, Jim's words mosey, as if he has all the time in the world to say what needs saying. He takes the basket and a blanket from Lucy's hands. She slides an arm into the crook of his elbow.

The pair amble the short distance to where Warm Springs and Rock Creek join, where the cottonwoods shade the summer trickle of water. The birds are now silent as the late-morning sun heats the prairie. A smart little breeze dances through the leaves, lifting Lucy's hair from her damp neck. An unexpected shudder runs her length. Jim tightens his arm on hers and smiles.

Jim flips the blanket out and smooths it over the grass, in the cool, speckled shade of the cottonwood. "Suppose I'll ever get you up off of this if I sit you down?" His face deadpan, Jim holds Lucy firmly by both hands and eases her to sit on the blanket.

Jim seats himself beside Lucy, removes his spurs and stretches his legs out before him. He is deliberate in unbuckling his gun belt, particular in folding it neatly about itself. "Ahem …" He clears his throat and begins picking at fuzz balls on the blanket.

In stark contrast to his quick, articulate mind, Jim's words form slowly. "Good Lord, Lucy, are you at all worried? I mean, do you know when you're due to birth? I don't have much experience. Haven't slept a wink since seeing you last Sunday for worrying. You shouldn't be here alone anymore."

"Did you bring the hog ties, then? Isn't that what you said? 'By God, I'll hog tie you, if I have to.' That's what I recall last February."

"This isn't a joke, Lucy. I was riled when I said that. With John getting shot, and you coming up missing, I'd ridden day and night to find you. I wasn't myself." Jim measures every word. "I want you to understand it doesn't matter to me when you and John … ahem … that's behind us. There will never be no judgement on that. I carry the blame. We both know it was foolish pride all the way around. Now, when are you due?"

"No sense trying to keep this conversation light, James." Lucy's breath hangs on his name. She prays under her breath, "Lord give me courage," and addresses Jim, "I have no secrets that you can't know. Not a one. John and I did not get together soon enough for this baby to be born until the end of August. He was your friend first, but he was mine, too. And he was here to save me after the beating. Jim, I would have died, and I grew to love John. That was after I thought you'd discarded me. Things were hard."

Jim leans back, pulling Lucy with him into the shade of the big log. She settles in, turning her tummy sideways, laying an arm across his belly and her head on his chest.

"To have your heart beating in my ear is like coming home," Lucy tells Jim. He sucks in a breath, draws her closer. She is surprised at her own tears.

They rest in the shade.

188

Jim begins his thoughtful precursor to conversation by clearing his throat. "Ahem … I surely owe John a debt. Lucy, you're so … so expansive, have you considered you might have two babies in there? Twins run in families and mighty strong in John's."

Lucy glances up at Jim. His brow is furrowed, as if he's been practicing how to approach her about the baby.

"Twins? Oh, heavens no," Lucy warbles, "Wouldn't that be something! One for the each of you. A Curry and a Thornhill." Jim flinches and Lucy smiles apologetically, "I wish I hadn't said that, but 'expansive,' really?"

"Darn it, Lucy, can't you see, I'm struggling here?"

"Forgive me," she laughs. "I've just never been called expansive before."

"Let me finish, before you pick at me. It's been a difficult year for us. If you are going to have twins, they could come at any time. I've inquired about it with Doc Clay," Jim admits. "He says you need to be near a doctor. I am not going to rest until you're where I can watch you. Understand?"

"Yes Jim, but to ease your worry, I assure you, it's not twins. It is one, strapping, left-handed boy, and his name is Harvey."

Jim's deep, throaty chuckle vibrates his chest. "Oh, for heaven's sake, that's just crazy enough to be true. Boy or girl, I'll be mighty pleased." He tightens his arm about her. "Two or one, you are going home with me. That's where it lies then." He chuckles again.

"Yes, I believe I am ready to go home, James Thornhill. So, are you taking me?"

"I am," Jim states. "We got us some catching up to do. Shall we eat and get along for the ranch?"

Lucy struggles to sit upright. Jim, trying to be delicate, is no help at all. He has no idea where to place his hands. Boyish and shy, he chuckles uncontrollably. "Lord, as familiar as I used to be with you, I'm feeling a bit lost."

Jim rises and turns to kneel over her. Lucy laughs until she's weak. "I've just become too darned expansive, that's it."

Jim places his hands under Lucy's arms and lifts her to a sitting position. "Lord, but you are a handful," he sputters.

"Aren't I, though? Good thing you're a strong man." Lucy opens the basket and sets out two cans of tomatoes. "Open these, please," she says and smirks at him while handing him the opener.

"Our favorite meal!" Jim exclaims, and peels the lids back, standing a spoon in each can. His face is consumed by the pleasure her remembering brings.

"Seems to be one of the few things I can eat these days, and it always reminds me of us."

"So, I have been on your mind?"

"I've found myself near chanting your name while going about the work of the homestead. James, Jim, Jimmer, my warm fire, my cool water, dusk, dawn, and everything in between," Lucy sings out in a tease. "Yes, perhaps, you have been on my mind. Some."

"And you on mine, day and night, and every minute in between," Jim laments quietly. "Ahem … now, here's what I'm considering, Lucy. I'll throw my saddle in your little spring-board wagon, we'll use your harness on Luc—ahem—on my mare. We'll lead your horse behind. Most of my boys have gone to Malta for the Independence celebration. It'll be a few days before they wander in. I'll bring a crew back to get your things when I round them up."

Jim lays out his plans, as they walk back from the creek. "Better bring with you what you need for a long spell. I'll get to readying horses while you gather your necessities."

"What's your mare's name?" Lucy suddenly inquires.

Jim's head jerks up, stopping short of looking at her. "Why do you ask?"

"Names are important. The pretty mare you ride, I've noticed she's the apple of your eye."

"The mare? Yes, she's a good one. Ahem … there's no denying it." Jim shakes his head, still avoiding Lucy's eyes.

"What else, James? What's her name, really?"

"Oh, darn it Lucy, you're backing me in a corner, and you know it." Jim glances off at his grazing mare. He coughs and stalls. "Lucy—I've called her Lucy. There! You might as well know it." The months of anguish flash across Jim's face as he talks. "She was to be a gift. The name was just until John brought her to you. I considered her a salve for John and I in settling our hard feelings. Turns out, me calling her Lucy was our last laugh together. After the shooting that morning, when the buckskin mare returned home, I had to bury John. I'd lost you both. I never had the heart to change the mare's name."

Lucy slips her arm into Jim's. "I don't have much to gather at the house. Can I walk with you?"

"I'd be pleased with that." Jim speaks softly as he sets the picnic basket in the wagon and picks up the shafts to roll it away from the fence.

Lucy strokes the mare's silky neck as Jim unsaddles her. "What a golden and dappled hide," Lucy admires. "It reminds me of the sun shining through the cottonwood leaves of autumn. She's beautiful, Jim." As if understanding the compliment, the mare gives her head a majestic toss.

Jim smiles and nods, "I'm rather fond of her." He loads his gear in the wagon. It takes him considerable time to adjust Lucy's old harness to fit his fancy mare. To Lucy, watching Jim's quiet, articulate ways is a reminder of why she loves him.

Lucy halters her own horse, tethers him to the back of the wagon, and pauses, studying Jim again. His hands are strong and quick, and at the same time slow and deliberate in their movements. John's words come to Lucy's mind, *That darn fussing is one of ol' Slow Jimmer's secrets. He is lightning with a gun, good at everything he does.*

Jim seems even slimmer at the waist than when Lucy last allowed herself the pleasure of looking. "My God," she utters under her breath, "you are the finest example of a man I have ever known."

Jim catches Lucy watching him and flashes his warm smile. "Maybe you should name this wild cat. She is yours, after all." He picks up the lines to back the mare between the shafts.

"I already have," Lucy declares. "I call her Sunday. Would you like to know why?"

Jim stops midway in his hitching, his brow arched into a question. "I suppose I would, Lucy," he hesitates, "unless you're going to poke fun at me again." And he gives his little head nod as he finishes hooking the traces.

192

"I believe it all started back February first." Lucy fully intended to poke fun, but words began choosing themselves.

"James, time seems to have taken on a backward circle since John's murder. Maybe everything started the night you and I strolled in the moonlight and you offered to protect me from Daniel. Told me you'd heard of his abuse. That was in the fall of '92, wasn't it? You'd ridden in looking for your friend, John. I'd just met him that morning, and he lay unconscious on my porch. I'd held the angels at bay all day digging buckshot from what was left of his right arm."

Jim lays the harness lines across the mare's back and leans over her, silent and motionless as he listens.

"But how could we outguess what would happen after that?" Lucy lets out a long sigh, "Oh, Jim, the day after John was killed, when you loped out of here on your big black horse, I was so terribly angry with you, with life, really. Then you showed up, again and again. Just like you promised you would. Each time, you were spit-shined, as if for a special occasion, and you began riding the mare. I'd never seen you ride a mare. I'd rarely seen you dress up or go to church. But that's what it felt like to me. Something holy."

Lucy walked to the mare, leaned across its back to rest her hand on Jim's arm.

"It soon became clear to me you were coming every Sunday. I began counting my ordinary days between Sundays, marking my life by the ringing of your mare's shod feet on the frozen creek bed. Then, after the thaw, it wasn't good enough to wait to hear you. I started standing on the little rise out west, by John's grave. From there, I'd watch the sun chase darkness from the rolling plains. A smile would wash over me when you topped the ridge. It would be my first all week. When you drew closer, I'd hurry back to the house. I couldn't let you catch me waiting." A silent sob escapes her. "When you would leave, I'd pray to live one more week. Pray to make it to Sunday next."

Lucy chances a look at Jim's face. His warm, earthy eyes are damp and dark at their rims. He moves his arm from her grasp and reaches to tilt his hat back. Fingers twist at a strand of the mare's mane. "God A'mighty, Lucy, had I only known," Jim whispers.

Genesis
by Patricia Frolander

You are my Adam, made of gumbo, rock, and wind.
Scarred bold hands confirm your labor,
back slightly bent, you lean into the land.
Shadowed canyons crevice your cheeks,
worry and laugh lines corner your eyes.
Shorter steps, shorter breath, but enough
to reach my arms.
I am your Eve, your rib, your thorn,
and always your love.

Authors of the Bearlodge Writers

Bjornestad, Kathy (Belle Fourche, SD) - Kathy Bjornestad is a retired educator, Labradoodle lover, and sometime-musician who found her forever home in the Black Hills. She has published several essays in *Christian Science Monitor Weekly,* as well as a picture book, *Rhymes from the Reef.* A middle-grade novel, *The Amazing Sunny York,* is forthcoming.

Bowers, James (Spearfish, SD) - James Bowers (B.A. Dartmouth College, M.A.R. Yale University, M.A. University of Redlands) has taught English at universities in the U.S., Finland, China, and Lithuania. His published works are essays in anthologies, a collection of short stories, and a study of Henrik Ibsen's early plays.

Bowers, Jytte Holst (Spearfish, SD) - Jytte Holst Bowers was born in Denmark and raised during the German occupation of World War II. Her published essays are in anthologies. Her memoir is *Freedom's Candles: From Tiananmen to Vilnius.* Unpublished works include translations from Danish and Norwegian, a book about her son, and some short stories and children's tales.

Brewer, Constance (Gillette, WY) - Constance Brewer's poetry has appeared in numerous magazines and anthologies. She is the editor for *Gyroscope Review* poetry magazine and the author of *Piccola Poesie: A Nibble of Short Form Poetry.* Constance is a big fan of Welsh Corgis, weekends, and white-line woodcuts. Find out more at constancebrewer.com.

Callan Rogers, Morgan (Bath, ME) - Morgan Callan Rogers came west in 2010, living in Spearfish, South Dakota, for five years, and joining Bearlodge Writers Group in Sundance, Wyoming. Morgan is the author of two books, *Red Ruby Heart in a Cold Blue Sea* and *Written on my Heart.* She lives in Bath, Maine, now, but misses the beauty and the friends she made out West.

Eastman, Maria Lisa (Hyattville, WY) - Maria Lisa hails from Hyattville, WY. She holds a Master's degree in Range and Watershed. The 2018 recipient of the Neltje Blanchan Award from the Wyoming Arts Council, she was awarded a 2019 scholarship to attend Billy Collins' workshop in Key West. Her poetry arises from the landscapes of Wyoming.

Frolander, Patricia (Sundance, WY) - Wyoming Poet Laureate Emeritus, Patricia Frolander manages the family ranch in the Black Hills. Patricia's recent release, *Second Wind*, received the 2020 Wrangler Award from the National Cowboy and Western Heritage Museum and Spur Award for Best Poem from that collection given by the Western Writers of America.

Gutiérrez, John R. (Gillette, WY) - John Gutiérrez, a first generation Mexican-American and a native of Wyoming, is a retired Spanish teacher of 31 years and a member of Prairie Pens and Bearlodge Writers. John writes fiction, creative non-fiction, and dabbles in poetry. His inspiration comes from Juan Rulfo, Rodolfo Anaya, Jorge Luis Borges, and Isabel Allende.

Helmer, Jean (Belle Fourche, SD) - Jean "BJ" Helmer writes flash non-fiction, liturgy, and poetry drawn from her roots in High Plains' agriculture, classrooms, and pulpits. A past-director of Dakota Writing Project's Summer Institutes, this educator/pastor has been published in *Watershed,* WyoPoets 2020 Chapbook; in *Pasque Petals, 2022;* in *Gyroscope Review,* and in *Before the Amen.*

Hummel, A.M. (Hulett, WY) - Originally from Florida, A. M. Hummel now "plays with words" from her home in Wyoming. A novel is in progress. She enjoys animals, editing for others, and reading and writing history, poetry, and magical realism. With a background in public relations, she has bylined in newspapers and regional magazines nationwide.

Moseley, Holly (Camp Crook, SD) - Holly Moseley started life in Michigan and moved west, finding her home on a ranch in South Dakota. Her poetry has appeared in *South Dakota Magazine*, several issues of *Pasque Petals*, and anthologies published by the Black Hills Writers, the Belle Fourche Writers, and WyoPoets.

Newland, Dawn (Colony, WY) - Dawn Newland is the author and illustrator of the historic novel series, *Of Men and Horses*. As a rancher living in the corner of Wyoming near Belle Fourche, SD, she has spent a lifetime immersed in the cowboy culture she writes about. She is an artist, and writer, of frontier America.

Peterson, Viktoriia (Sundance, WY) - Viktoriia Peterson, originally from Ukraine, has lived in Wyoming for eight years. She completed online courses in Creative Writing and has published three children's books; a poetry collection, *A Breeze of Inspiration*; and a thriller, *Karlik from Planet Sirius*. Her pseudonym is DoLoraVi.

Roseland, Bruce (Spearfish, SD) - Bruce Roseland ranches in South Dakota. Books include *The Last Buffalo*, 2006 (Wrangler Award); *Prairie Prayer*, 2008 (Will Rogers Award); *Church of the Holy Sunrise*, 2012; *Song for my Mother*, 2014; *Gift of Moments,* 2016; *Cowman,* 2018 *(*Will Rogers Award*)*; *Heart of the Prairie,* 2021. (Will Rogers Award). Roseland is a past president of the South Dakota State Poetry Society.

Smith, Kathleen (Gillette, WY) - Kathleen Smith's home is on the Little Powder River in northeast Wyoming. Generations of family shaped her love of rivers, hayfields, and cow pastures. She cares for ranch lands following her legacy and writes about the reality of ranch life.

Endnotes

Part One: Forge New Courses

Bowers, Jytte Holst. "War, Peace, and Marriage." *Freedom's Candles: From Tiananmen to Vilnius*, Chapbook Press, 2021, pp 1-6.
Frolander, Patricia. "Bittersweet," *Writers' Digest* Poetry Contest, Fifth Place, 2014.

Part Two: Echoes of Distant Voices

Brewer, Constance. "Encompassing Noise." *Anti-Heroin Chic*, 2021.
Frolander, Patricia. "Dream Watch." *Second Wind*, High Plains Press, 2020. [American Poetry Foundation Selection, 2020]
Roseland, Bruce. "You Are Born into Someone Else's Story." *Scurfpea Anthology*, Scurfpea Publishing. 2022
Frolander, Patricia. "Piper Dream." *Gyroscope Review: Winter Edition*, 2021.

Part Three: Bittersweet

Brewer, Constance. "Given Wings." *Sheila-Na-Gig,* 2020.
Bjornestad, Kathy. "Truth Will Rise," *Wyoming Writers Newsletter*, July 2022. [Flash Fiction Winner]

Part Four: Pierce the Fog

Frolander, Patricia. "Baptism." *Second Wind*, High Plains Press, 2020. [Winner of the Western Writers of America Spur Award]
Helmer, Jean. "Prom Night." *Oakwood*, South Dakota State University Press, 2019.
Helmer, Jean. "Diving into Grief." *Pasque Petals*, vol. 90:9, South Dakota State Poetry Society, 2022.

Part Five: Illusion of Control

Newland, Dawn. "The Legend of Old Blue" *Of Men and Horses*. *Arizona Tough,* The Cowgirl Historian, April 2022, pp 293-300.

Bjornestad, Kathy. "Summer Birds on the *Albion*," *Scribes Valley Anthology*, First place, Oct. 2014.

Frolander, Patricia. "Recessive Jeans." *Between the West Pasture and Home*. Self-published, 2021.

Part Six: Thrum of Contentment

Bjornestad, Kathy. "Waiting for Thimbleberries." *The Christian Science Monitor Weekly*, 12 August 2012.

Brewer, Constance. "Unexpected Grace." *Kosmos Quarterly*, 2021.

Part Seven: Together Is a Compliment

Brewer, Constance. "Love Poem with Accolades." *Kosmos Quarterly*, 2021.

Brewer, Constance. "The Family Rate." *Door Is A Jar*, 2021.

Newland, Dawn. "The Sunday Mare" (revised excerpt). *Arizona Tough: Of Men and Horses*, The Cowgirl Historian, April 2022.

Frolander, Patricia. "Genesis." *Married into It*, High Plains Press, 2011.

Index

Acknowledgments

Cover Art by Sarah Rogers

Sarah Rogers was born in Seattle, Washington. Her school-aged years were divided between the Black Hills and Florida. Desiring to be a neurosurgeon, she enrolled in the University of Florida where she soon discovered their art school. After receiving her BFA from the University of Florida, Sarah moved to South Carolina where she worked as a graphic designer. Next, it was on to New York for a decade as a Madison Avenue art director for a small creative advertising agency.

Sarah's style of painting shows the influence of her background in graphics. The paint-line (appearing or disappearing), its color and space (positive or negative) is the subject. The paint and how it moves is the focus. While she chooses traditional subject matters and mediums, Sarah uses them in a non-traditional manner, working on smooth surfaces so the paint makes its own textures. Rogers applies several layers of pigment to achieve the strong colors that characterize her work. She paints on clayboard with a well-used toothbrush and other tools. This allows her to create her own textures. The clay surface lends itself to scrubbing, lifting, and otherwise removing pigment and reapplying it to create a variety of surfaces.

Rogers states, "Each of us has an inner existence that calls for expression, and we find joy and gratitude in that expression. My perceptions are expressionistic and somewhat abstract. My work is very personal, and I truly love what I do. Henry Miller said, 'to paint is to love again, and to love is to live life to the fullest.'"

The Bearlodge Writers are honored to have Sarah's work grace both our anthologies. Her extensive philanthropy is well known in the Black Hills region. What a blessing to share her work, appreciate her patronage, and call her friend.

Cover Design and Consulting
by Constance Brewer:

A special thank you to Constance Brewer, editor of Gyroscope Press, for her spectacular cover design and spot-on advice.

Bearlodge Writers:
P.O. Box 204 Sundance, Wyoming 82729
bearlodgewriters@gmail.com

Gyroscope Press
PO Box 1989
Gillette, WY 82717
gyroscopepress@gmail.com